Set Free

Penetrating the Darkness of the Masonic Lodge

Richard Ford

Unless otherwise noted, all Scripture quotations are taken from the *King James Version* of the Holy Bible.

Oaths of obligations and other references of the secret works of The Lodge are quoted from memory by the Author.

Masonic order and procedure quotations - *Lightfoot's Manual of The Lodge* (c) 1934, used by permission, *The Grand Lodge of Texas, Ancient Free* and *Accepted Masons.* Noted by L.M.L. where indicated.

Negro Lodges: The laws of The Grand Lodge of Texas A.F. & A.M. Effective December 1959 - Revised 1972. Prepared and published by Authority of The Grand Lodge. Chapter 5 - Title 1 - Juridiction and Power. ART. 15. (15) - Page 71
Noted by L.G.L. where indicated.

Definition of Masonry - The Catholic Bible Dictionary. The Catholic Press, Inc. Chicago: Illinois 1960 - Page 154.
Noted by C.D. where indicated.

Albert Pike statement on masonry - Chick Publication, Chino, California (c) 1978, used by permission.
Noted by C.P. where indicated.

Front Cover Photo Credit: www.shorsburgh@horsburgh.com

ISBN 1-931600-55-4

First Printing 2003

Published by Family Worship Center
910 Brand Lane
Stafford, Texas 77477
Phone: 281/499-0551
Website: www.thefwc.org
Email: FGF@wt.net

——— ··· DEDICATION

My heart cries for the multitudes that have been and are being deceived by the Masonic Order. Those involved in the Blue Lodge, Shrine, Scottish Rite, Eastern Star, Rainbow Girls, DeMolay Boys and many more that have branched from this organization.

It is with great love and concern that I dedicate this book to a people that are truly seeking to become better people, seeking not only to better themselves, but to also reach out to help others. Their desire for enlightenment is honorable, their motives are sincere, but like as I was, they are searching for truth and light in the wrong place.

How my heart breaks when I encounter someone involved in this deception because they are blinded and in bondage and don't know it.

As so often has been quoted by those who lost their personal freedom and gained it back later, people such as P.O.W., those wrongly accused and sentenced for crimes they did not commit, etc., each one seems to proclaim upon their release the same basic statement, "You don't realize the true value of freedom until you lose it."

So it is with myself and others who have broken free from the bondage of Masonry. "I did not know how bound I was until I was .....

Set Free!

CONTENTS

FOREWORD
by Dr. Morris Cerullo

Richard Ford is a unique man of God.

God has anointed him as pastor and worldwide apostle, and he carries a distinctive prophetic gifting.

His personal testimony "Set Free" goes forth with a powerful, driving objective - receive it, and what happened to Richard Ford can and will happen to you. God is no respector of persons.

Be Set Free!

Dr. Morris Cerullo
President
Morris Cerullo World Evangelism

—— ··· FOREWORD
by Dr. Charles E. Blair

I first met Pastor Richard Ford in Lagos, Nigeria a few years ago. We were both part of the teaching team of the School of Ministry sponsored by Morris Cerullo World Evangelism.

We were next door to each other in the hotel and shared transportation to and from the open arena where more than 40,000 leaders gathered from across the great continent of Africia. I soon learned that Richard had ministered several times over several years in this needy nation, and that he had a keen understanding of the awesome responsibility facing us as trainers.

I looked forward to hearing him teach, and after his first session, I decided to attend each of his scheduled times because of his heavy anointing and special ability as a communicator handling God's Word. But that which ministered to me best and impressed me most was his ability to perceive and penetrate the source of spiritual forces, both good and bad, at work in various situations.

Since that eventful experience in Nigeria, we have

shared the pulpit and platform in various places, occasions I have both looked forward to beforehand and thoroughly enjoyed while together.

When I received the *Set Free* manuscript, I better understood the source and the force of this man's free spirit, as well as the power available to free the spirit of others held in the grip of bondage.

Don't make the mistake of just reading Richard Ford's story as it were just his story; but rather focus on the secrets...the principles...the nuggets of truth it contains that not only set *him* free, but that are able to produce the transformation and power to set others free.

Richard Ford was not only delivered, but he became a deliverer. And through this powerful expose`, you too can learn to know those principles, experience them in your own life, and then teach them to others also.

Dr. Ford experienced the force of bondage, but once he discovered the source of that evil force, he was able to change his course by changing the source. And thus he is the man of God that he is today.

His story is a truly great one and speaks for itself. It was written for you and me to know the Source, to experience the force whose source is God, and then to become a channel through which others will be set free.

But beyond that, it conveys through practical life experience the tremendous truth that there are no secrets in what God can do. His wonder-working power is available to everyone - Richard Ford, me, you, your circle of influence. That's the secret of the gospel. It gives light and not darkness; freedom, and not bondage. Anyone can be *Set Free!*

Dr. Charles E. Blair
Pastor Emeritus, Calvary Temple, Denver, CO
President, Blair Foundation

⟵ ···FOREWORD
by Dr. Jerry Savelle

Pastor Richard Ford has been a personal friend of mine for many years.

His deep commitment to the call of God upon his life and his enthusiasm for seeing the captive set free is a joy to behold.

In his new book "Set Free - Penetrating The Darkness Of The Masonic Lodge", you'll sense his compassion, his sincerity and his tremendous desire for people to know the truth. It's only truth that can penetrate the lies of Satan and Pastor Ford certainly puts the devil in his place in this powerful book.

If you know anyone who has been deceived by things that seem to be of God but are not, then please get this book into their hands.

Jerry Savelle
Jerry Savelle Ministries
Crowley, Texas

⟶ ··· INTRODUCTION

You are about to embark on a journey of life and faith, a glimpse into my life at a time when I was searching for truth. A time when I needed something good in my life.

You might say, "Why didn't you turn to God and the church?" And I am sure after reading this book you will say , "How could you be so naive to get involved?"

My answer? Backslidden and blinded by sin, turned off to church by what I thought was a place filled with a bunch of hypocrites; yet I of all people was the most hypocritical.

Satan , the master of deception, saw me stop my forward motion toward hell and to ensure that I would not find God and His delivering power, and my God destiny, led me in a direction which he assumed would render me non-threatening. An organization with the appearance of good, but...full of deception - The Masonic Order.

I am sure of one thing, the devil will use anything he can to prevent you from finding the truth. Yes, he will even use religion and God. Go to church, sing all the right songs, but don't believe and apply the truth. I've often said, "The devil cares not whether you go to heaven or hell. His concern is that if you do not serve him on this earth then do something else, anything as long as you do not find the true power of God; for it's then the battle will rage as you will have become a threat to his kingdom and purpose."

Little did I know that my journey would be interrupted by God, a power released to open my eyes, deliver me and empower me to turn and set the captives free. A journey that would show me "God is Greater". Greater than all the powers of darkness! Greater than the plans of the devil!

When God gets on your trail there is no place to hide. **His pursuit will result in His Purpose**! His purpose was to call me, appoint me and anoint me for my life's work. Serving Him, pastoring His people, destroying strongholds and setting captives free; literally plundering hell and populating heaven.

Throughout the Bible we read about men and women who dared to move under the anointing of the Holy Spirit to do what God told them to do, even when all the circumstances seemed to point to defeat. That kind of disciple is fearless and bold as they go about setting the captives free and turning the world upside down.

For this to be accomplished, there must be a place or event, something that can be used as Holy Ghost University. Yes, God will invade your life and use what you are involved in to strengthen and train you to serve Him. Turning natural events into supernatural encounters. *(Acts 9)*

Looking back, I can see that God was teaching me to overcome fear, controlling spirits, and how to pull down strongholds of the mind. Calling me to discipleship, preparing me to move under the anointing, fearlessly facing the enemy with boldness, running to the battle with no quitting sense, and turning the world upside down.

As we begin our journey together, please keep in mind I am not striking out at people. This is not a personal attack on those involved in masonry.

"For God sent not his Son into the world to condemn the world; but that the world through him might be saved." (John 3:17)

Yet, we must never lose site of the fact that He also came to seek and destroy whatever stood between Him and His divine mission; whether it be religion, man made organizations, doctrines, traditions or satanic influences. (Mark 7:13, Acts 10:38)

I am speaking out and sounding an alarm against

false religions, organizations, doctrines, traditions and satanic plans. Those that deny the one true God, the God of Abraham, Isaac and Jacob. The God and Father of our Lord Jesus Christ.

Many seem to think it's proper to recognize all religions, to fellowship with them, to pray with them; to say, "We all worship the same God, we are all going to heaven, so let's all get along."

We must respect the dignity of all men, we must respect their right to believe as they will. Yet, as Christians, we must not involve ourselves in worship and prayer with those who deny Jesus.

Befriend them? Yes! Social interaction? Yes! But at the same time standing firm and bold as a voice for the Lord. (Ezekiel 33:8) Declaring there are not many gods, there are not many ways to heaven.

There is only one God - Jehovah! (Exodus 20: 1-3)

There is only one way - Jesus! (John 14:6)

"Do you believe that Jesus is the only way? Will people go to hell because they don't believe He is the only way to salvation?" We will be confronted with those questions by non-believers, friends, co-workers, etc. They might not ask those questions in such frank language, but nevertheless the questions will remain. Our response must be, "Yes, **Jesus is the only way!**"

We will be marked as religious bigots. We will be mocked and yes, even persecuted as being politically incorrect and intolerant. But, sound the alarm we must!

Bam! Bam! Bam! The sound of light exploding into darkness. The sound of an invasion. The Holy Ghost invading spirits of darkness to set captives free.

I was that captive! Bound in sin, bound in the darkness of ignorance, longing to be free. Searching for peace and guidance; but searching in all the wrong places.

You hold in your hand an incredible story - a true story. A story of God's grace, mercy and delivering power.

You hold in your hand knowledge. Knowledge empowered by revelation which will be a weapon of destruction to the rulers of darkness.

As any writer must, I have dug into the enormous and ever-growing mass of information available as I walked through masonry. But I write not from a scholarly position, but from a first hand experience, so that the general reader will not be burdened with arguments which led to my exposure of this cunning trap set by Satan.

I have introduced nothing that cannot be supported from the evidence available. I have aimed at authenticity rather than conjecture, to prevent the imagination from roaming at the cost of reality.

Masonry is a real threat - I have sounded the alarm. I have opened the door so light can shine in. I have broken the shackles of bondage, of deception - now the captives can be **Set Free**!

Read it slowly, read it carefully, read it prayerfully, it is God's anointing to equip you to set the captives free.

Multitudes are deceived and bound by the Masonic Order and its different branches. Sincere, good people, truly seekers of truth and goodness. But like as I was - deceived.

Deceived by the Master of deception, Satan. The Master of deception will use any and everything at his disposal to keep humanity from finding true Light. The Light from heaven, Jesus and His redeeming power.

Today in the hands of Satan are many tools of deception, one of those is the Masonic Order.

Darkness veiled in light to deceive, delude and to place in bondage, humanity.

"And no marvel; for Satan himself is transformed into an angel of light." (II Corinthians 11:14)

The one disguised as an angel of light, slowly, but surely leading people into darkness and bondage.

As you walk through a page of history in my life through this book, I have this assurance, that the eyes of your understanding will be enlightened and you will see through the surface of the Masonic Order and into the depths of its deception. (Ephesians 1: 17-22)

Then go forth and minister grace and deliverance to those whom you will encounter that are captives of darkness through the Masonic Order.

As I have said, it's a page of history in my life. God stepping into my life to turn me, to position me for my destiny. A life that was filled with everything but God. But God!

How God suddenly invaded my life, delivering me from darkness into His marvelous light. Taking an auto parts salesman and turning him into a Pastor.

From influencing people in a worldly way to the pathway of God.

Little did I know that all of this was going to be used by God to develop me to Pastor a great church. Nor could I have ever imagined that I would travel the world setting the captives free. It was my destiny calling!

Listen - your destiny is calling!

Someone is on the road to Damascus. (Acts 9) Sincere in their travels, truly believing they're on the road of good works.

Yet like Saul, truly going in the wrong direction.

Suddenly!

A light from Heaven, an invasion of the Holy Ghost sent to expel darkness and deception. Turning Saul into Paul.

As you go and encounter the Sauls of life, release the true light of Jesus Christ and the delivering power of the Holy Ghost - the results?

Suddenly Saul will be transformed into Paul!

It's then you will hear His voice..."well done good

and faithful servant, enter thou into the joy of the Lord."

As you go remember our battles are not with people, but with evil spirits of darkness.

Our purpose is to open their eyes to the truth.

My prayer is that as you go, all of those with whom you will encounter will truly be ......

Set Free!

CHAPTER ONE

Devil's Honcho

As a youth my parents saw to it that I was trained within the atmosphere of the church. Even though I was under the influence of the church, I was rebellious.

I grew up in the Stafford-Missouri City-Sugar Land, Texas area.

Even though I was rebellious and full of mischief, the Word of God was penetrating my life. My parents sent me off in the summer to live with my grandmother. She attended services Sunday morning, Sunday night, Wednesday night, and all the services in between, at a Baptist church in Little River, Texas. Grandmother took me to Vacation Bible School and exposed me to more of the Word of God. The Bible says in Proverbs 22:6, *"Train up a child in the way he should go: and when he is old, he will not depart from it."*

Little did I know that the seed of godly training and prayers would one day explode into a full blown harvest in my life.

Not only did my parents and grandmother (mom's mom) give me godly training, but I had a grandfather (dad's dad) that was a Baptist Pastor. Even though I did not see much of him during my formative years, because he lived a great distance from us, I know that he called my name out to God on a regular basis.

As I look back, I have often wondered about something. He had a nickname for me that really made no sense. He called me "Peter Boy". Why would you call a child named "Richard", "Peter Boy"? You don't suppose this wise Pastor saw his only grandson acting like Peter in the Bible - do you?

Rambunctious, wild, disorderly, boisterous, unruly! You don't suppose that he was making comparisons between my character and the character of Peter - do you? Surely he didn't proclaim to God that in spite of my uncontrolled zeal, that one day I would have an encounter with God like Peter, that would thrust me into service for God.

You don't suppose he would look at me and say "Thou art ... but thou shalt be!"

Peter before his encounter with God was one of instability, his parents called him Simon (blown with the wind like a reed); yet, Jesus saw into his future and called him "Peter" (part of a rock). Someone gave me a plaque with the name "Richard" on it with the interpretation of the name "Powerful Ruler."

You don't suppose my grandfather would look at me and say, "Yes, you act like Peter now but you shall become a powerful ruler." Do you suppose God gave this godly Pastor a glimpse into the future of his only grandson? Even though he died before I answered the call of God, do you suppose God answered his prayer anyway? I wonder?

The Lord says His Word shall not return unto Him void. I was taught the Word of God in Sunday School and church. In a youth revival, when I was 9 or 10 years old, the Holy Spirit revealed to me the need for Jesus in my life. I got up, walked the aisle at the Stafford Baptist Church, and gave my heart to Jesus. Yes, the same church I would someday pastor. Later I was baptized at Missouri City Baptist Church. In my teenage years my parents and I went to church together. After I entered high school, for whatever reason, my parents ceased to go to church as often and relaxed their rule and hold upon me. I began to drift.

A time comes in each person's life when they are faced with the decision of standing upon their own faith. But my selfishness became the dominant thing in my life and overrode God's will for me. No one can live our life for us. No one but God can change us, and sometimes the old sinful nature rises up within us and takes control. Thus, I drifted and went out into the world of sin.

During my high school years I became more rebellious and was in and out of trouble, and walked deeper and deeper into the pits of darkness. In fact, I totally walked away from God.

Arrested in April 1958 for breaking and entering a local grocery store, stealing soft drinks and food for our beach party during the Easter holidays.

16 years old and already experienced in sin. Smoking, drinking, malicious mischief of every kind. Trouble looking for a place to happen.

One night in jail taught me one thing. You don't want to go to jail again - ever! I was glad that all I had been doing in the past had not caught up with me or I might have never gotten out of jail.

Even though I was not recognizing God in my life, God was watching over me. What could have resulted in jail time, resulted in probation.

In spite of all my meanness and hard heartedness, I always knew that God was God and that my life depended on Him; yet, I would not yield to His pull on me.

Also, I knew that Jesus Christ was the King of kings and the Lord of lords, but I would not allow Him to be the Lord of my life. I had gone over to the devil's side and began to do his work. I became the **Devil's Honcho**.

In 1959 I married my wife Tena. She's still my wife to this day. As a young couple we walked through the world and the pleasure of sin and the temporary joy that it brings. We became caught up in the party-ing circuit of dancing and drinking. Because Tena and I were the instigators of most of the partying, people flocked to us. We led many people in the wrong direction. Later, God brought most of those people back to us and allowed us to tell them we were wrong, and then we shared the Word of God with them. Many were saved.

Tena and I continued our walk in the world still not recognizing God. Somehow, I always was aware of an unfulfilled need in my and Tena's life. The Word of God says that Jesus never leaves nor forsakes us. He was always there patiently awaiting as we walked into sin. Today we realize His hand was all around us.

I went into business for myself in the early 60's, and began to work seven days a week, twelve and four-teen hours a day. I began to make money, and **money became my god**. The Bible says the **love of money** is the root of all evil. My love of money was deeply rooted into evil. While trying to gain the world I was losing my soul.

I watched my family deteriorate, as I tried to give them every material possession that I had never had. For lack of knowledge and responsibility being taught them, my children destroyed the things that I gave them. Money was spent like it came from an open faucet. When I was around, no one's money but mine was good. My marriage and my life began to fall apart because I had pitched my tent with the enemy.

Drinking excessively, my very existence depended on beer joints, taverns and nightclubs. Although I had been in and out of fights all over this country, shot at and had broken beer bottles and knives pulled on me, I have never been cut, shot or beaten. I walked with the authority of Satan and, I too, destroyed. Being number one head honcho in the devil's army, I had no fear of death or anything around me. Even though I was serving the devil, he tried to kill me.

One night, after I left a beer joint, I was going down a stretch of road that I had traveled many, many times. I knew it like the palm of my hand because we had lived in that area for over ten years. As I was going down that road it was as though there was a plan from Satan to take my life. It seemed as though the devil himself grabbed the steering wheel of my El Camino, and as long as I live, I shall never forget what transpired.

I felt a hard jerk on the steering wheel to the extreme left. I was doing probably 75 or 80 miles per hour. The pickup veered off the road, went into a ditch and through a barbed-wire fence. At the moment I went through that ditch and hit the fence, I said, "Oh, my God, I'm going to die." How odd that I would cry out to God, you see for over 10 years, all I ever asked God to do was "damn" everything that got in my way. Yet instantly, the Word of God came alive in my life. Romans 10:13, *"For whosoever shall call upon the name of the Lord shall be saved."*

When I cried out to the Lord, I believe in my heart and I know it with my spirit that the angels of the Lord reached down and shoved me over to the passenger's side of my automobile. The El Camino went through the fence, across the pasture two to three hundred yards, right up on the edge of a tremendously deep drainage ditch, 25 or 30 more feet, the pickup turned and came back out into the pasture and went directly back to the very spot where I entered into the barbed wire before. A post and other entanglements wrapped around the drive shaft had stopped me from moving. When the pickup stopped,

I was on the passenger's side - I sat there speechless and very sober.

I stepped out to check the damage. The pickup started but would not move, I needed to find out why. Wow! 40 foot of wire and post trailing behind me. Then I heard a voice, "Hey man, there's no road out there." I looked up and a V.W. Bug had stopped on the side of the road. A man was sitting on the front end drinking a quart of beer watching the whole thing.

I walked over to him, asked for a lift back down the road to my brother-in-law's house in hopes of getting help and a ride home. As I opened the door to get in, beer bottles rolled out. I got in and before I knew what happened, the car shot out onto the road bouncing from side to side. I thought, "Oh great, saved from my own wreck only to get killed in a yellow V.W. by a crazy drunk."

At the time, I laughed about it, but as the Lord began to reveal the truth to me, today I know that it was a plan of the devil to destroy me. I look back on that accident as the turning point in my life. My life of running from God had come to an end. Remember, **His pursuit will result in His purpose**. I realized then that I was on a road to total destruction, and I knew I had to get my life in order. I didn't know what to do but I tried in my own strength to pull the pieces together, trying to stay out of the beer joints, and cutting down on drinking and other things that were consuming my life, more time was spent with my wife and children. Tena and I never separated, yet there were times I'm sure she wanted to. But God had His hand on that woman for she never ceased to love me, pray for me, and never gave up on me. I praise God for that. Without the help of Almighty God and the spirit of that woman I would not be where I am today.

Searching for something good, I didn't turn to the church because all I could see was traditions and doctrines of men. I had all that I wanted of the world and their rules and regulations, and I didn't need anyone to tell me what I was doing wrong; I was well aware of my faults. Organized religion had no appeal whatsoever to me. Something good was needed in my life, and because of my desire to get close to something good, I was drawn into an organization about which I knew absolutely nothing.

Since I was not involved in fellowship with the body of Christ or the study of the Word of God, I could not prove or disprove the things that were being shown to me. If I had known the Word of God, I would not have become involved, for the Scripture says: *"Have no fellowship with the unfruitful works of darkness, but rather reprove them."* (Ephesians 5:11)

You Took the First Step

A young man who worked for me had joined the Masons and casually mentioned that he was doing what is called "petitioning" the Masonic Lodge. He was accepted and initiated into the Masons, and I became very inquisitive and asked him questions. He would only smile and tell me that he was not allowed to share because it was against the rules of the organization to do so. There were secrets that could never be shared with the outside world. All his statement did was stir more deeply the inquisitive nature within me to find out exactly what I was not supposed to know. If I had known the Word of God, I would have stopped right there, because again the Scripture says, *"Have no fellowship with the unfruitful works of darkness..."* (Ephesians 5:11)

I was impressed by one of the things he said. "Let me name you some men who are Master Masons, and you'll see that they are good and upright men." Truly they were. As he named many men in our local community, I saw a picture of good men - which drew me closer to Freemasonry. Remember, I needed something good in my life.

I asked, "How do I become a Mason? How do I join?"

"You just did," he said. **"You took the first step - you asked."**

Masons believe that you must ask to be a Mason. You must come of your own free will and ask. And I did!

The Lodge sets up a committee of men who are designated and delegated to visit and question the candidate. One of the first things you must do is to fill out a petition which has been recommended by several Masons in good standing of the jurisdiction of the Lodge in which you intend to join. I had no problem getting those men to sign my petition, although my reputation was one that had much to be desired.

The investigating committee came to my home and business and questioned my moral obligations and reasons for joining. Needless to say, they were satisfied because I was accepted to be initiated into the Masonic order.

My initiation was set for April of 1971. That night I was very excited and nervous - nervous because I was standing at the door of an unknown organization where little light had shown forth.

The things that had been presented to me appeared

wholesome. I had no fear of what I was going into. As I was being prepared for initiation a series of things were read to me from **The Lightfoot's Manual of the Lodge**.

Entered Apprentice
PREPARATION OF THE
CANDIDATE

"When the candidate of initiation shall have entered the preparation room, the Secretary of The Lodge, or some other officer or member, shall, by direction of the W.∗. M.∗. repair thither, and may address him as follows:

Mr. _____, somewhat of your motives, in applying for admission into our Ancient and honorable fraternity, we have learned from the declarations contained in your petition, over your signature. It now becomes my duty to recall to your memory some of the more important promises and declarations you have made therein, and each of which, we find you have answered in the affirmative:

1. You have promised upon your honor, to strictly adhere to and be governed by the Constitution and Laws of the Grand Lodge of Texas, and by the By-Laws of this Lodge.

2. You have sincerely declared, upon your honor, that unbiased by friends and uninfluenced by mercenary motives, you freely and voluntarily offer yourself as a candidate for the Mysteries of Masonry.

3.   You have seriously declared, upon your honor, that you are prompted to solicit the privileges of Masonry by a favorable opinion conceived of the institution, a desire for knowledge, and a sincere desire to be of greater service to your fellowman.

4.   You have seriously declared, upon your honor, that you, will cheerfully conform to all the ancient established usages and customs of Masonry.

5.   You have seriously declared, upon your honor, that you firmly believe in the existence of God; the immortality of the soul; and in the Divine authenticity of the Holy Scriptures.

You are again reminded of these solemn declarations, because they constitute important considerations upon which the Lodge acted, in looking with favor, upon your request to be admitted a member among us.

In order that you may not be misled as to the character or the purpose of the ceremonies in which you are about to engage, the Lodge addresses to you these preliminary words of advice.

Freemasonry is far removed from all that is *trivial, selfish,* and *ungodly.* Its ceremonies are by no means of a light or trifling character, but are of profound significance and deep solemnity. They have existed without material changes from remote antiquity. Its structure rests upon the indestructible foundation of the Fatherhood of God, the Brotherhood of Man, and the Immortality of the Soul.

Our ancient and honorable fraternity welcomes to its doors, and admits to its privilege, worthy men of all faiths and creeds who possess the indisparable qualifications. Freemasonry is, in one of its major aspects, a beautiful and profound system of morality, veiled in allegories and illustrated by symbols. Its grand purposes are, to diffuse light; to banish ignorance; to promote peace and happiness among mankind; to relieve distress; to protect the widows and orphans of your brethren; to inculcate a wider knowledge concerning the existence of the Grand Architect of the Universe, and of the arts and sciences connected with His Divine laws. In fine, the design is to make its members wiser, freer, better, and consequently happier men.

These purposes are accomplished by means of a series of moral instructions taught, according to ancient usage, by allegories, symbols, types, figures, and lectures.

With this brief and general explanation, is it still your desire to proceed?

If the candidate answers in the affirmative, then continue:"

I declared that it was, because I really didn't even comprehend what was being asked of me. There was no way I could retain what he had spoken to me. After I said "Yes" he proceeded further:

"As a preparation for the mystic rites into which you are about to enter, you will now be asked to divest your mind and conscience of all mental prejudice and superfluities incident to a material or worldly life; and to remember that selfish aims and vanities, if present, are not in keeping with the reverential spirit which a true seeker of Divine Light and Wisdom must manifest when he enters upon the path of true initiation. I will now leave you in the hands of true and trusty brethren, who will attend to your further preparation and see that you proceed as all others have done who have gone this way before." [1]

At that point I was asked to disrobe and take off all metallic substances within my possession. They placed upon me a pair of pajama-type pants with the left leg cut off at the knee. **I was blindfolded and a cable tow, a length of rope**, **was tied around my neck.**

They had me in a room separate from the main room, as I stood there, there was a knock at the door. The door was opened. The man outside spoke: "Who comes here?"

The man standing at my right, that was taking care of me, was doing the answering for me. He said, "Mr. Ford, **a poor, blind candidate who desires to be brought from darkness to light** by receiving a part of the rites, lights, and benefits of this worship Lodge of free and accepted Masons, erected to God and dedicated to the Holy Saints John, as all worthy brothers have done who have gone this way before him."

The man inside asked me, "Mr. Ford, is it of your own free will and accord you make the request?"

I declared that it was.

He turned back to the man beside me saying, "Brother Master of Ceremonies, (not the same as Worshipful Master) by what further rights does he expect to gain admission?"

He answered, "By being a man, free born, sound in mind and members, and coming under the tongue of good report."

Later I learned the meaning of "by being free born." The Masonic Lodge is prejudiced against black people. They will not allow them within the Masonic Order. I quote from **The Laws of the Grand Lodge of Texas A.F. & A.M. Effective December 3, 1959. Revised 1972 Prepared and published by**

authority of the Grand Lodge.

Title 1 - Chapter 5 - Juridiction and Powers. ART. 15. (15) - Page 71

"Negro Lodges. This Grand Lodge does not recognize as legal or Masonic any body of Negroes working under any character of Charter in The United States, without respect to the body granting such Charter, and they regard all Negro Lodges as clandestine, illegal and un-masonic; and moreover, they regard as highly censurable the course of any Grand Lodge in The United States which shall recognize such bodies of Negroes as Masonic Lodges."[2]

Even though men of color have their Masonic Lodges, they are not affiliated with the Grand Lodge of Texas. I suppose that out of desperation or even spite toward the white race, their Lodge was conceived. I do not know any of the history of their Lodge, yet I know that they are very similar to the lodges dominated by the white race and the bondage is the same. I have had several opportunities to share with men of color when I notice their Masonic involvement. There is one thing I am sure of, **Satan is color blind**.

Also, I understood later what was meant by "sound in mind and in members." There is no place in the Masonic Order for anyone that has a mental incapacity or if you have any member of your body missing due to an accident, birth defect, or whatever the cause may be, only in extremely rare cases will they ever admit anyone with these handicaps. I know of no one that was not physically whole, especially hearing and the parts of the hands because of a secret word and grip that must be given to recognize one Mason as another.

Another prejudice became evident as I moved deeper into Masonry. The Lodge #1141 in Sugar Land, Texas, to which I belonged and was initiated into was very prejudiced against Catholics. They would not allow Catholics to join. There were many rumors that Catholics had burned down Lodges, but this was purely malicious gossip.

I quote from the **Catholic Bible Dictionary**. **The Catholic Press, Inc. Chicago: Illinois 1960 Page 154 -** Masons: "An international fraternal organization which dates in its present form from the first quarter of the 18th century, and claims connection with similar organizations of pre-Christian times. Masons state the aim of Freemasonry as "work for the welfare of mankind" and claim to "strive morally to ennoble (dignify) themselves and others and thereby to bring about a universal league of mankind." (Emphasis mine.)

Catholics are forbidden under pain of excommunication to belong to the Masons. In the beginning, the Masons were largely anticlerical and were guilty of secret and open plotting against the Church and against civil governments. Freemasonry is also objectionable to Catholics because it is a religion of pure naturalism. Masons have their own beliefs about God, human morality, and the human soul. Moreover, they have their own religious rites. Catholicism, the uniquely true religion founded by Christ, therefore, is irreconcilable with Freemasonry."[3]

The Catholic church is one of the few churches that has taken a stand against Masonry. Through ignorance of the truth about Masons most churches hold this organization in high esteem.

Next I was told to wait until my request was made known to the **Worshipful Master** and his answer returned. At the time I didn't know what Matthew 23:10 says: *"Neither be ye called masters: for one is your Master, even Christ."* We are not to place ourselves as masters over any person. I had a problem when I became Master of the Lodge by being called "worshipful master" for I'm not worshipful of any and the master of none. There is one Master and only one to be worshipped: Jesus Christ and the Lord God Almighty.

After they closed the door and went through the ceremony of talking to the Master of the Lodge they returned, opened the door and asked me to enter. Inside the Lodge Hall (in the inner chamber), I was stopped and something sharp pierced my chest. A man in front of me spoke.

"Mr. Ford, you are received upon the point of a sharp instrument, piercing your naked left breast, which is to remind you that as this instrument is a torture to your flesh, so should the recollection be to your MIND and CONSCIENCE should you even attempt to reveal the secrets of Masonry to anyone unlawfully."

You'll notice this was an emotional experience dealing with the mind. The very thought and association of pain goes with the revealing of the secrets of Freemasonry. It has a brainwashing effect. It's mind-controlling. Associating pain with unlawfully revealing the secrets of Freemasonry. There are rules and regulations of how you may reveal things and then only to those that are members who have proven themselves to be so after trial and examination before you. Nevertheless it has a mind-controlling effect.

Then I was brought to the center of the Lodge room and told to kneel. The worshipful master placed his hand on my head and asked, "Mr. Ford, in whom do you place your trust?"

Immediately I said, "God", most men do, although actually it is not required in the Masonic Lodge. To be accepted you simply have to profess a belief in deity. Later I asked some of the "brothers" what would happen if a man refused to answer the questions properly. They said that was what the rope around the neck was for. If the person caused any problems, raised a raucous, or would not leave willingly, then the cable tow would be used to drag him from the Lodge room.

---

1 - L.M.L. - pg 7,8,9

2 - L.G.L. - pg 71

3 - C.B.D. - pg 154

NOTICE OF ELECTION

(To Candidate)

Sugar Land........., Texas, ... March 16........, 19 71..

To ... Mr. Richard Frank Ford..

Dear Sir:

I have the pleasure to inform you that at a Stated Communication of

......Sugar Land........Lodge No. 1141......, A. F. & A. M., held ...March...15, 19 71..,

you were elected to receive the Mysteries of Masonry in this Lodge.

Please present yourself for initiation on......Monday.............evening

......April...12.........., 19 71.., at......8:00...P...M.....o'clock.

Respectfully yours,

Andrew J. Blair

....Secretary.

Andrew V. Blair, Sec.

(SEAL)

Form No. 47—5M—10-65—Masonic Home Press.

43

CHAPTER THREE

In Whom Do You Place Your Trust?

There is a misconception in the statement "In whom do you place your trust". Most assume the answer to be "God". The God of the Christians, yet this is not the case. Whatever the belief system, it will be respected and accepted by the Masonic Lodge. Hindu, Buddhist, cult or whatever the designation of God, it is not required to be defined as most would suppose. Masons must fellowship with all religions.

Lightfoot's Manual of the Lodge, Chapter 14, entitled,

THE FURNITURE OF THE LODGE

"The Holy Bible, Square and Compasses are said to constitute the *furniture of the lodge*. They are, respectively, dedicated to God; to the Master of the Lodge; and to the Craft. The Holy Bible is properly called a greater light of Masonry, for from the center of the Lodge it pours forth from east to west and north to south its effulgent rays and divine truth. The

45

Bible is used, among Masons in this country, as the symbol of the Will of God, however it may be expressed; and, therefore **whatever expresses that Will may be used as a substitute for the Bible** in other countries; otherwise, Masonry would be a sectarian institution, incapable of universality. Thus, in a Lodge consisting entirely of Jews, the Old Testament alone may be placed upon the altar. Turkish Masons may make use of the Koran. Whether it be the Gospel to the Christians, the Pentateuch to the Israelite, the Koran to the Mussulman, or the Vedas to the Brahman, **it everywhere Masonically conveys** *the same idea* **- that of the symbolism of the divine will revealed to man**..."[4]. (Emphasis mine)

This shows you the deception of the Masonic Order.

Should a person who denies the deity and virgin birth of Jesus Christ say, "I believe in God", he is accepted into the Masonic Lodge. Only Christians believe that Jesus is God. I never heard the name of Jesus Christ mentioned during the years that I was in the Masonic Order. No part of the rituals, lectures or commentaries, or prayers mentioned Jesus. Most Scriptures are taken from the Old Testament. What few are used from the New Testament omit the name of Jesus Christ. II Corinthians 6:14 says, *"Be not unequally yoked together with unbelievers: for what fellowship hath righteousness with unrighteousness? And what communion hath light with darkness?"*

The Scriptures plainly forbid children of God, born-again believers to adhere to the previous statements of the Masonic order.

After I said that I placed my trust in God, I was told to stand up. My faith had been well-founded to follow my leader and fear no evil. I was led around the Lodge one time, stopping at each of the "stations" where the Lodge officers sit. The Worshipful Master sits in the east. The Junior Warden sits in the south. The Senior Warden sits in the west. No one sits in the north. Masons believe that the north is a place of darkness. At each station the questions were the same that I was asked at the door. The same answers were given.

I was then brought to the center of the Lodge and told that I was now before the **HOLY ALTAR OF FREEMASONRY**. The Worshipful Master of the Lodge was addressing me at this time. He arose and spoke these words: "Mr. Ford, you now stand before the holy altar of Freemasonry. Before you can proceed further, YOU MUST TAKE UPON YOURSELF AN OATH OF OBLIGATION WHICH I ASSURE WILL NOT INTERFERE WITH YOUR DUTY TO GOD, YOUR COUNTRY, YOUR NEIGHBOR, OR YOURSELF. With this assurance are you willing to proceed?"

Hearing the question and fully believing it to mean

what it said it meant, I declared that I was willing to proceed. Then I was told to kneel upon my naked left knee, my left hand supporting and right hand resting upon the Holy Bible, square and compasses. The Worshipful Master called the people of the Lodge to arise and form a circle or a line on either side of me. Then he stood before me and asked me to repeat the following oath of obligation for the Entered Apprentice Masons Degree:

"I Richard Ford, of my own free will and accord, in the presence of Almighty God and this worshipful lodge of free accepted Masons erected to God and dedicated to the Holy Saints John, do hereby and hereon sincerely and solemnly promise and swear that I will always hail, forever conceal and never reveal any of the secrets of Freemasonry to anyone unlawfully, except it be to a true and lawful brother, or within the body of a just and legally constituted Lodge, and not to him or them whom I may hereso to be, but unto him and them only whom I shall find so to be after strict trial, due examination, or lawful information.

I furthermore promise and swear that I will not write, indite, print, paint, stamp, stain, cut, carve, engrave, inlay, or enamel the same upon anything movable or unmovable under the canopy of heaven whereby the secrets of Freemasonry might be unlawfully attained, **binding myself under the penalty of having my**

throat cut from ear to ear, my tongue torn out by its roots, my body buried in the rough sands of the sea, a cable tow length from shore where the tide ebbs and flows twice in twenty-four hours, should I knowingly or wittingly violate or transgress any part of the Entered Apprentice Masons obligation, so help me God and keep me steadfast."

As I took the oath of obligation, it never registered with me what was being said or what I was repeating. I remember smiling as they said I would have my throat cut from ear to ear. I thought of that as funny and foolish. LITTLE DID I KNOW THE BINDING EFFECT ON MY MIND. Again the fear of death and pain were associated with the revealing of the secrets of Masonry. How unscriptural! A binding, blood oath before Almighty God! How could such a horrible thing be asked of a man? But it was, and blindly I walked into it. Had I known the Word of God, immediately I would have known to leave. *"But I say unto you, Swear not at all; neither by heaven; for it is God's throne: Nor by the earth; for it is his footstool: neither by Jerusalem; for it is the city of the great King. Neither shalt thou swear by thy head, because thou canst not make one hair white or black. But let your communication be, Yea, yea; Nay, nay: for whatsoever is more than these cometh of evil."* (Matthew 5: 34-37)

"What? know ye not that your body is the temple of

the Holy Ghost which is in you, which ye have of God, and ye are not your own? For ye are bought with a price: therefore glorify God in your body, and in your spirit, which are God's. " (I Corinthians 6:19-20)

Imagine swearing a binding oath of obligation that I would have my throat cut from ear to ear!

I was told to arise, then led to the northeast corner of the Lodge room. The Master of the Lodge spoke to me: "Mr. Ford, you now stand before this Lodge a just and upright Mason. It has been the custom of this Lodge that a man after having passed through initiation as you have just done, that he be required to deposit with the Master of the Lodge a metallic substance. Have you anything of a metallic nature about your person that you can deposit with me at this time?"

At that moment I thought of my wedding ring, but it and all metal had been removed from me. I stood with the most humble feeling of my life. Then a man in the audience gave me a metal object. I felt very grateful to him.

The Worshipful Master spoke to me again: "Mr. Ford, this is not done to trifle with your feelings, but it was to teach you a very important lesson in Masonry. Should you at anytime meet with anyone, more especially a brother Mason, in so destitute a state as you just were, it will be your obligation to come to his relief as readily as this brother did to you."

I was then given further explanations of the emblems of the First Degree of Masonry.

I was led out of the Lodge, into the anti-room, given my clothes, brought back into the Lodge, stood before the altar and addressed by the Worshipful Master. "Mr. Ford, the brethren are satisfied as to your physical qualifications. They now desire to test your mental qualifications to see if you can recall any portion of our ceremony which strikingly impressed you. You will be escorted to the secretary's desk where you will be furnished suitable writing material, and given the opportunity to write any portion of our ceremony which may have strikingly impressed you." Then he added, "Brother Master of Ceremonies, lead the brother to the secretary's desk."

I was taken to the secretary's desk, furnished with a sheet of paper and a pencil. As I sat there with my mind reeling with the things that had previously transpired, I could not comprehend any portion or retain anything. However, I wanted to make a good impression.

I thought of the word "Bible" and touched the pencil to the paper and made one small mark, when the man next to me brought his hand down upon the desk with tremendous force. The paper was jerked out of my hand. I was jerked to my feet and pushed in front of the Worshipful Master.

The man standing next to me said, "WORSHIPFUL MASTER, THE BROTHER IS ATTEMPTING TO WRITE THE SECRETS OF MASONRY."

Fear gripped me. The Master that night was a friend of mine. He was doing a good job of the part that he was playing during the ritual, because he looked very hurt and disgusted as he looked at me and said, "Mr. Ford, do you not recall that just a few minutes ago you **knelt before the holy altar of Freemasonry and swore that you would never write the secrets of Masonry**? Yet, in such a short time we find you violating that obligation!"

I answered, "Yes."

"Mr. Ford, this is not done to trifle with your feelings but was to remind you that the secrets of Freemasonry are never to be written. From time immemorial my brother, the secrets of Freemasonry have been handed down from generation to generation and lodged within repository of faithful breast."

Those present laughed, then shook my hand, and I officially became an Entered Apprentice Mason of

Sugar Land Lodge #1141. I was well on my way to becoming very involved in Masonry.

CHAPTER FOUR

Secret Works

I was told that Masonry was not a totally secret organization because all of the rituals and much of the Masonic order is recorded on microfilm in the archives at Washington D.C. Masonry is not a secret organization but an organization with secrets. Many of our presidents, senators, congressmen and high officials have been Masons. Masons proudly proclaim that George Washington, Gerald Ford and others were Masons.

All the teachings of Masonry or what is called "the secret work," that is, the rituals of the installation of a candidate, the ceremonials of initiation, the rituals of opening and closing the Lodge, and the different degrees are all secretly taught by word of mouth from one man to another, while spending countless hours in his home, automobile, or wherever, that he may be able to obtain the information and commit it to memory as it is repeated to him.

The repeating of the consequences associated with the revealing of any information, produces fear. Your mind becomes programmed. As a child is taught that a stove or lighted match is hot, he learns to associate pain with heat. Instantly he knows not to touch because he has been taught that a hot object is painful. So does Masonry teach its members the association of fear of death and pain with the revealing of its secrets.

After I had been initiated as an Entered Apprentice Mason, I was given a lecture concerning the emblems, symbols and allegories surrounding the Masonic order.

I will only share with you a few of the many things they taught me during the lecture. As you read them you will see the subtleness of Masonry as it begins to program the mind of its candidates. As it does with the oaths of obligations.

THE COVERING OF THE
SYMBOLIC LODGE

"The covering of the Symbolic Lodge is no less than a clouded canopy, or starry-decked heavens, where all good Masons hope at last to arrive, by the aid of the theological ladder which Jacob, in his vision, saw ascending from earth to heaven; the three *principle* rungs of which are denominated *Faith*, *Hope* and *Charity*; and which admonish us to have faith in God, hope of immortality, and charity to all mankind.

Of these, *Charity* is the greatest; for Faith may be lost in sight; Hope end in fruition; but *Charity* extends beyond the grave, through the boundless realms of eternity."[5]

As you read these things you will begin to see more and more how **Masons are taught that a moral, just life brings eternal salvation and immortality**. Rather than the shed blood of Jesus' atonement.

The lecture mentioned "where all good Masons hope at last to arrive." One cannot work his way to heaven by living a good life. Ephesians 2:8-9 says, *"For by grace are ye saved through faith; and that not of yourselves: it is the gift of God: Not of works, lest any man should boast."*

Furniture

The Entered Apprentice lecture continued with explanation of the furniture of the Lodge.

"THE FURNITURE OF THE LODGE is the Holy Bible, Square and Compasses.

* * * * * *

The Holy Bible is dedicated to God, because it is the inestimable gift of God to man: * * * * * the Square to the Master, because it is the proper

Masonic emblem of his office; and The Compasses to the Craft, because, by due attention to their use, they are taught to circumscribe their desires and keep their passions within due bounds."[6]

Note the asterisks in the above quote. These asterisks appear in the manual, but when spoken over a candidate during their initiation the following statement is inserted. "upon the Bible we obligate the Mason." This again has an effect upon the mind. Should one desire to share about Masonry, the thought of his having sworn before God with his hand on the Bible causes him to stop short of completely sharing all he knows. He feels that in so doing he has gone against God. FEAR keeps him from sharing.

Dedication

"Our ancient brethren dedicated their Lodges to King Solomon, because he was our first Most Excellent Grand Master; but modern Masons dedicate theirs to St. John the Baptist, and St. John the Evangelist, who were two eminent patrons of Masonry; and since their time, there is represented, in every regular and well-governed Lodge, a certain *Point within a Circle*, embordered by two perpendicular parallel *lines*, representing St. John the Baptist, and St. John the Evangelist; and upon the top rests the Holy Scriptures. The point represents an individual brother; the circle is the boundary line, beyond which he is never to suffer his prejudices or passions to betray him.

In going round this circle, we necessarily touch upon these two lines, as well as the Holy Scriptures; and while a Mason keeps himself circumscribed within these due bounds, it is impossible that he should materially err."[7]

A deception of Masonry is that it encourages one to believe that King Solomon, John the Baptist and John the Evangelist were patrons of Masonry, and since their time Masonry has transpired. Masonry did not evolve in the time of John the Baptist or the building of King Solomon's Temple. King Solomon was not building a Lodge hall for Masons and John the Baptist was NOT preaching or teaching the beauty and splendor of Masonry, or how to live a good, moral life so one could go to heaven. Matthew 3:2 says he was preaching *"...Repent ye: for the kingdom of heaven is at hand."* Nowhere in the Scriptures does it say that John the Baptist or John the Evangelist were Master Masons, nor does it condone such nonsense.

At the conclusion of this lecture the following charge was given to me:

CHARGE

"My Brother: _____ As you are now introduced into the first principles of Masonry, I congratulate you on your admission into this ancient and honorable Order; ancient as having existed from time immemorial; honorable, as tending to make all men so, who are strictly obedient to its teachings and precepts. No institution was ever raised on a better principle or more solid foundation; nor were ever more excellent rules and useful maxims laid down, than are inculcated in every Masonic Degree.

There are three great duties which, as a Mason, you are charged to inculcate - to God, your neighbor, and yourself. To God, in never mentioning his name but with that reverential awe, which is due from a creature to his Creator; to implore His aid in all your laudable undertakings, and to esteem Him as the chief good. To your neighbor, in acting upon the square, doing unto him as you wish he should do unto you; and to yourself, in avoiding all irregularity and intemperance, which may impair your faculties, or debase the dignity of your profession. A zealous attachment of these duties will insure public and private esteem.

As a citizen, you are to be a quiet and peaceable subject, true to your government, and just to your country; you are not to countenance disloyalty or rebellion, but patiently submit to legal authority, and conform with cheerfulness to the government of the country in which you live.

In your outward demeanor, be particularly careful to avoid censure or reproach. Let no interest, favor or prejudice, bias your integrity, or influence you to be guilty of a dishonorable action.

Your prompt attendance at our meetings, when at labor in the Entered Apprentice Degree, is earnestly solicited; yet it is not meant that Masonry should interfere with your necessary vocations, for these are, on no account, to be neglected; neither are you to suffer your zeal for the institution to lead you into argument with those who, through ignorance, may ridicule it. At your leisure hours, that you may improve in Masonic knowledge, you are to converse with well informed brethren, who will always be as ready to give, as you will be to receive instruction.

Finally, keep sacred and inviolable the mysteries of the Order, as these are to distinguish you from the rest of the community, and mark your consequence among Masons. If, in the circle of your acquaintance, you find a person desirous of being initiated into Masonry, be particularly attentive not to recommend him unless you are convinced he will conform to the laws, customs and usages of the Order; to the end, that the honor, glory and reputation of the Institution may be firmly established, and the world at large convinced of its good effects."[8]

When I had "turned in my work" for the Entered Apprentice degree, I was brought before the regular meeting of Master Masons, seated in the middle of the Lodge room where I was questioned. I answered word for word, without hesitation or error, exactly how they had taught me. Very little error is permitted. Answers are to be given as near letter perfect as it was taught. What was meant by "turning in my work" was simply to go back over my initiation and explain it in detail.

I was quickly passed by the Lodge as being proficient. My second degree, the Fellow-Craft, was set to be given to me.

---

5 - L.M.L. - pg 24
6 - L.M.L. - pg 26
7 - L.M.L. - pg 32,33
8 - L.M.L. - pg 37,38,39

CHAPTER FIVE

Further Light

The second degree is called Fellow-Craft. A predetermined date was set for a called lodge meeting, to confer upon me the Fellow-Craft degree.

I was led into the anti-room, stripped of my clothing and metallic substance. I wore the same type pajama bottoms as in the first degree - with the exception that this time the right knee was naked and the left knee covered, the **cable tow removed from my neck** as in the first degree and **placed around my right arm**.

The same procedures were followed as in the previous degree, of being led by the Master of Ceremonies up to the door, and the door being knocked upon. Once again, as in the first degree, basically the same questions were asked, except for a few minor changes.

One of the basic changes was that as the Master of Ceremonies knocked upon the door, the man asked, "Who comes, who comes here?". The question was asked twice instead of once because it was the second degree into which I was being initiated.

The Master of Ceremonies answered the question for me: "Brother Richard Ford, who desires FURTHER LIGHT in Masonry, as all worthy brothers have done who have gone this way before him." I was called a brother because I had passed the first degree, but I still had more to go. Thus the statement - **Further Light**.

The man inside asked if my work had been turned in, properly received, voted on and passed. The answer was "Yes". Again the same basic question and answer series was presented - until we stepped inside the Lodge Room.

As we entered, the man inside halted me and spoke, "Brother Ford, you are **received upon the angle of a square applied to your naked right breast**," (In the first degree the left breast was pressed with the point of a compass.) "which is to remind you to square your actions upon the square of virtue toward all mankind more especially a brother Mason."

The second degree is very similar to the first as far a being escorted around the Lodge Room, except this time I went to each station twice. Similar questions were asked.

Again I declared I was willing.

I was told to kneel on my naked right knee, my left knee forming a square, my right hand resting on the

Holy Bible, square and compasses, my left arm extended forming a square, supported by a square.

The Worshipful Master asked me to repeat the obligation:
"I Richard Ford, of my own free will and accord in the presence of Almighty God and this Fellow-Craft Masons Lodge do hereby and hereon sincerely and solemnly promise and swear as I have heretofore done with these additions; that I will not communicate the secrets of this degree to anyone except it be to a true and lawful brother, or within the body of a just and legally constituted lodge, and not to him or them whom I may hereso to be but unto him and them only whom I shall find so to be, after strict trial, due examination, or lawful information.

I furthermore promise and swear to stand to and abide by the rules and regulations of this or any other Fellow-Craft Masons Lodge of which I may become a member.

I furthermore promise and swear to answer and obey all due signs and summons handed or sent to me from a Fellow-Craft Mason Lodge or a brother Fellow-Craft Mason, if within length of my cable tow.

I furthermore promise and swear to help aid and assist all brother Fellow-Craft Masons of this or any other Fellow-Craft Masons Lodge.

I furthermore promise and swear that I will not cheat a Fellow-Craft Masons Lodge or a brother Fellow-Craft Mason out of the value of anything, knowingly, nor permit it to be done if within in my power to prevent it, all of which I solemnly promise and swear to keep and perform without the least equivocation, mental reservation, or secret evasion of mind; **binding myself under the penalty of having my left breast torn open, my heart and vitals taken thence and cast as a prey to the vultures of the air and beasts of the field**, should I knowingly or wittingly violate or transgress any part of the Fellow-Craft Masons obligation so help me God and keep me steadfast."

Even though I was told I was being taken further into light, you can see that the opposite was true. With each step, I was being taken deeper and deeper into the grip of darkness and bondage.

I was told to arise, then was led before the Worshipful Master and presented with what is called the working tools of a Fellow-Craft Mason.

THE WORKING TOOLS OF A
FELLOW - CRAFT
* * * * *

"This section closes with the moral explanation of the *Plumb, Square* and *Level.*

The Plumb is an instrument made use of by operative Masons to raise perpendiculars; the *Square* to square their work; and the *Level* to lay horizontals; but we as free and accepted Masons, are taught to make use of them for more noble and glorious purposes; the Plumb admonishes us to walk uprightly in our several stations before God and man, squaring our actions by the Square of Virtue, and remembering that we are traveling upon the Level of Time, to "that undiscovered country, from whose bourne no traveler returns". ,

Again a form of godliness was presented but the truth is that we are not traveling to an undiscovered country. Masonry teaches UNCERTAINTY because it does not have the truth - UNCERTAINTY because it teaches that by morality and goodness you will obtain everlasting life in heaven. This is unscriptural. The Word of God is full of truths about the rewards in heaven and the rejoicing of the saints, but they are promised only to those who accept the shed blood of Jesus.

The second degree of Masonry, Fellow-Craft deals with what is called the liberal arts and sciences. The degree was conferred with two pillars standing inside of the door which goes into the five orders of architect. These are: Tuscan, Doric, Ionic, Cothinthian, and Composite. The five human senses are brought out in this lecture: hearing, seeing, feeling, smelling and tasting. Three of the five are revered by Masons; namely, hearing, seeing and feeling:

HEARING that they might hear the word of a Master Mason; SEEING that if they should see the sign given they should fly to the relief of a brother; and FEELING that they may know the grip of a Master Mason.

HEARING, of course, is to hear the secret passwords of each one of the degrees. The passwords are: the Entered Apprentice Degree-Boaz; in the Fellow-Craft Degree Jachin and Shibboleth; and for a Master Mason - Tubal Cain and Maha-Bone. These words are known throughout the world and must be spoken, thereby showing the importance of hearing. If you are deaf you cannot be a Master Mason.

SEEING, so you may see the distress signal - something that is known among every Master Mason - that of raising the hands above the head, then bringing them down in three motions: 1) From the fully extended position over the head and saying "Oh Lord". 2) Bringing the hands down to a position level with the shoulders and repeating, "My God". 3) Bringing the hands down before you as if to receive something in the hands and saying, "Is there no help for the widow's son?".

As one progresses on to the Master's Degree this unfolds in the rituals of Masonry as the DEATH, BURIAL, and RESURRECTION of Hiram Abiff, the widow's son of the tribe of Naphtali in the Old Testament. During the initiation this is reenacted as everyone stands around Hiram's grave and the same words are spoken which is considered the NATIONAL DISTRESS SIGN. The importance of seeing to a Mason is that he should go to the aid of his brother.

FEELING, that which is used by Masons to identify the grip. He grips the hand in a normal handshake, in the First degree. He places his thumb upon the first knuckle of the other man's hand and the other man does likewise, and pass the word to each other; thus each man recognizes the WORD and the GRIP.

The Fellow-Craft grip is similar except that the thumb is upon the second knuckle as the word is passed. The grip of a Master Mason is locking of one's hand around the other man's wrist. This is called the strong grip of the Lion's Paw of the tribe of Judah. And that's how Masonry implies the widow's son was raised from the dead.

Again, at the end, a charge was given to me as a Fellow-Craft Mason:

CHARGE TO THE CANDIDATE

"My brother: Being passed to the degree of Fellow-Craft, permit me, in the name of the brethren, to congratulate you on your preferment. The internal and not external qualifications of a man are what Masonry regards. As you increase in knowledge you will improve in social intercourse.

It is unnecessary to recapitulate the duties which, as a Fellow-Craft, you are bound to perform, or to enlarge on the importance of strict adherence to them, as your own experience and examination will convince you of their value.

Our laws and regulations you are strenuously to support, and be always ready to assist in seeing them duly executed. You are not to palliate or aggravate the offenses of your brethren; but, in the decision of every trespass against our rules you are to judge with candor, admonish with friendship and reprehend with justice.

The study of the liberal arts and sciences, that valuable branch of education which tends so effectually to polish and adorn the mind, is earnestly recommended to your careful consideration; especially the science of Geometry, which is established as the basis of our art.

Geometry, of Masonry (originally synonymous terms), being of a divine and moral nature, is enriched with the most useful knowledge; which it proves the wonderful properties of nature, it demonstrates the more important truths of morality.

Your past behavior, and regular deportment have merited the honor which we have conferred; and in your present character it is expected that you will conform to the principles of the order, by steadily persevering in the study and practice of every commendable virtue. Such is the nature of your engagement as a Fellow-Craft, and to these duties you are bound by the most sacred and solemn ties".[10]

Again, the form of godliness, yet denying the power thereof. That concluded the Degree, and as before, I learned my question and answer series, was brought before the Lodge, turned in the work and was declared proficient.

The sublime degree of Masonry was before me - that of Master Mason.

---

9 - L.M.L. pg. 44, 45
10 - L.M.L. pg. 67,68

CHAPTER SIX

MAHA-BONE

The final and most important degree in Masonry was set for me: the Master Mason. The time was approximately six months after I had first been accepted into Masonry, which is extremely fast. I poured my heart into it. My dad had taught me that I should always give my best. So I endeavored to do all that was in my power to be a good Mason. I studied, worked and denied myself everything that I could for it. The final degree was now before me.

I was brought to the Lodge, stripped of my clothing and all metallic substances. This time both knees were out of the pajamas, which left me in a shorts-type affair with a **cable tow around my waist**. The degree was briefly explained.

Master Mason

"Freemasonry as before stated, is progressive, and a knowledge of its philosophy and teachings can only be acquired by time, patience, perseverance and close application.

In the first degree, we are taught the duties we owe to God, our neighbor and ourselves.

In the second, we are more thoroughly inducted into the mysteries of moral science and learn to trace the goodness and majesty of the Creator, by minutely analyzing His works.

But the third degree cements the whole, and is calculated to bind men together by mystics ties of fellowship, as in a bond of fraternal affection and brotherly love.

It is among the brethren of this degree that the Ancient Landmarks of the Order are preserved, and it is from them the rulers of the Craft are selected. It is in the Master's Lodge that all business of a legislative character is transacted and all balloting takes place..." [11]

Again being blindfolded and led to the door, three knocks were made upon it, indicating that this was the third degree in Masonry. Again the man inside asked who I was.

The Master of Ceremonies said, "Brother Richard Ford, A Fellow-Craft Mason who desires MORE LIGHT in Masonry." It was **LIGHT** the first time, **FURTHER LIGHT** the second, and **MORE LIGHT** the third time. One is not fully and openly accepted into a Masonic Lodge until you have completed all three degrees.

Again the same basic question and answer series was spoken until we stepped inside the Lodge Room. As we entered the man inside halted me and spoke: "Brother Ford, you are received upon the points of the compass extended from your naked right to your naked left breast, which is to teach you to circumscribe your desires and keep your passions within due bounds."

I was led through the Lodge Room, while circling it three times. Questions were asked which were similar to the other degrees. As I was brought before the altar I was told by the Worshipful Master that I again stood before the holy altar of Freemasonry, and as before, I could not proceed until I took a solemn obligation, which they assured me for the third time that it would not interfere with my duty to God, my country, my neighbor, or myself. I was asked if I was willing to proceed. Each time a Mason is brought into the Lodge to be conferred with a degree, the binding of the oath gets deeper and deeper.

I was told to kneel before the altar, my hands were placed upon the Holy Bible, again I was told to repeat the oath of obligation:

"I, Richard Ford, in the presence of Almighty God

and this Master Mason's Lodge do hereby and hereon sincerely and solemnly promise and swear as I have heretofore done with these additions: that I will not communicate the secrets of this degree to anyone except it be to a true and lawful brother or within the body of a just and legally constituted Lodge and not to him or them whom I may hereso to be, but unto him and them only whom I shall find so to be after strict trial, due examination, or lawful information.

I furthermore promise and swear to stand to and abide by the rules and regulations of this or any other Master Mason's Lodge of which I may become a member.

I furthermore promise and swear that I will stand to and abide by the constitution, resolution, and edicts of the Grand Lodge of Texas or any other Grand Lodge of which I may become a member.

I furthermore promise and swear to answer and obey all due signs and summons handed or sent to me from a Master Mason's Lodge or from a brother Master Mason, if within length of my cable tow.

I furthermore promise and swear I will not hold unlawful Masonic communications with a suspended or expelled Mason knowingly, nor permit it to be done if within my power to prevent it.

I furthermore promise and swear to keep the word of a Brother Master Mason when communicated to me as such, murder and treason alone excepted and these left at my option.

I furthermore promise and swear that I will not defile the good name of a Brother Master Mason nor permit it to be done if within my power to prevent it.

I furthermore promise and swear I will not be at the making of a Mason of an old man in his dotage, a young man in his nonage, an atheist, a libertine, a mad man, a bondsman, woman, or fool, knowingly, nor permitted to be done if within my power to prevent it.

I furthermore promise and swear that I will not set in a Clandestine Lodge, a suspended or expelled Lodge, knowingly, nor permitted to be done if within my power to prevent it.

I furthermore promise and swear that I will not cheat, wrong, or defraud a brother Master Mason or a Master Mason's Lodge out of the value of anything; knowingly, nor permit it to be done if within my power to prevent it.

I furthermore promise and swear to help, aid, and assist all poor and penniless Master Masons, their widows, and orphans.

I furthermore promise and swear that I will not violate the chastity of a Brother Master Mason's wife, widow, mother, sister, or daughter; knowingly, nor permit it to be done if within my power to prevent it.

I furthermore promise and swear that I will not communicate the word of a Master Mason in any other manner than that which I shall hereafter receive it.

I furthermore promise and swear that I will not give the sign of distress unless I am in actual distress, real danger, or for instructions; and should I see the sign given or hear the word accompanying it, I will fly to the relief of the brother giving the same should there be a greater probability of saving his life than losing my own.

All of which I solemnly promise and swear to keep and perform without the least equivocation, mental reservation, or secret evasion of mind, **BINDING MYSELF UNDER THE PENALTY OF HAVING MY BODY SEVERED IN TWAIN, MY BOWELS TAKEN THENCE, AND BURNED TO ASHES, AND THE ASHES SCATTERED TO THE FOUR WINDS OF HEAVEN,** that there might not remain among men or Masons trace or recollection of so vile a wretch as I, should I knowingly or wittingly violate or transgress any part of the Master Mason's obligation, so help me God and keep me steadfast."

Surely you can see the bondage that is upon the lives of Masons! Masons' wives and children have no earthly knowledge of what they are involved in because secrets are not to be revealed.

Let's go over a few of the things that were in the Master's obligation so you can recognize the tremendous binding that is on the mind and life of a Master Mason. HE IS LITERALLY UNDER BONDAGE TO THE LODGE. He promises to stand by the rules, regulations, constitution and resolutions and obey all the summons that are sent to him or handed to him, placing him in total submission to the Lodge.

The oath says that I would keep the word of a brother Mason when communicated to me as such, **murder and treason alone excepted**. A Master Mason is bound by oath, should he see him committing any crime he is bound not to tell. He is bound to lie in a court of law. He is bound to never, never, ever, ever go against that brother. Murder and treason alone excepted, and those are left to his option.

Note the oath, which says that he will not defame the good name of a brother Master Mason. One may talk about anybody but never against a Master Mason.

The Freemasonry person vows he will never be at

the making of a mason of an old man in his dotage, of a young man in his nonage (one must be 21 years old to enter into the Masonic Lodge), of an atheist, or a libertine, mad man, boundsman, woman or fool. Women cannot be Masons, neither can those who are mentally incapacitated or handicapped. He'll not sit in a clandestine Lodge or suspended or expelled Lodge. A clandestine Lodge is any Lodge not recognized by the Texas Grand Lodge. The Master Mason vows to not knowingly cheat a brother Master Mason out of the value of anything.

Notice that it always says **knowingly** - which is an escapism. If he doesn't know it, I suppose he can do it.

The oath says that he won't violate the chastity of a brother Master Mason's mother, sister, wife, widow or daughter. But, here too it says **knowingly**. It didn't say anything about anyone else's mother, or sister, etc., it merely said of a brother Master Mason.

Bondage in all of its fury was released into my life. I thought I had completed my Master Masons initiation, but such was not the case. My journey had just begun.

---

11 - L.M.L. - pg 68

CHAPTER SEVEN

HOODWINKED

I was led out of the Lodge Room. I dressed in my normal clothing, and then they placed a jewel on me. This jewel was placed around my neck. I was told that I was an honored guest and to wear it proudly. (I took that hook, line and sinker.)

I was seated in one of the officer's chairs. I sensed something wasn't right, but didn't know what. The Lodge was called back to "labor" to conduct business. The Master looked at the Tiler (keeper of the door) and asked him if he would go to the brother sitting in the South (which was me) to see if I was in possession of the secrets of a Master Mason. I figured something was haywire, but didn't know what.

As the Tiler came to me he smiled cordially, extended his hand. I, of course, gripped his hand with all the confidence in the world. He Said, "My Brother, can you give me the grip of a Master Mason?" It dawned on me that he had not yet given me the grip.

I said, "No," and as I said that he violently jerked his hand away from me. It was all an act, but it was to impress me with fear of not knowing what I was doing, and not ever reveal secrets if I had them, or pretending to have them if I didn't. Then the Tiler looked back at me with a stern look and asked, "Can you give me the word of a Master Mason?" Of course, I couldn't. He stormed away, walked to the door and slammed it. He looked at the Master of the Lodge and said, "Worshipful Master, the Brother in the South is not in possession of the secrets of a Master Mason."

The Master went through a ceremony of really rebuking the man for allowing someone into the Master's Lodge without the word or the grip of a Master Mason. "Brother Junior Warden, what caused you to ever think that the Brother in the South was in possession of the secrets of a Master Mason?"

"Worshipful Master," replied the Junior Warden, "the brother came in with other brethren whom I knew to be Master Masons. I saw he was clothed as such and I supposed him to be in possession of the secrets of a Master Mason."

"You supposed him to be in possession of the secrets of a Master Mason, when one of the first things you are taught is that the internal qualification and not the external qualification recommends a man to be made a Mason." Then he continued by saying that he should be more careful and permit only those to enter that know the word and the grip and had his permission.

He then turned to me and said, "My Brother, you doubtly supposed that you were in possession of all the secrets of a Master Mason, but it is my duty to inform you that such is not the case. **You have yet a rough and rugged road in which to travel, a journey in which life has been lost. You will permit yourself to be HOODWINKED, taken to the altar where you'll be given an opportunity to pray."**

I didn't know what was going on - mental anguish gripped my mind. I had supposed I was now a full-fledged Master Mason in possession of that degree's secrets. Instead, they reblindfolded (hoodwinked) and carried me to the altar.

I was told to arise when I was through praying. When I arose, men on both sides grabbed me and began to run with me. This is where the candidate becomes the acting part that supposedly Masonry is established upon. That is the building of King Solomon's Temple and Hiram Abiff, the widow's son of the tribe of Naphtali in the Old Testament.

They led me and did the speaking as they brought me to each of the Lodge's three stations. These stations are: the Junior Warden, the Senior Warden, and the Worshipful Master.

They stopped and a man slammed his foot on the floor. He put his hand against my chest stopping me and said, "Grand Master Hiram Abiff told us that at the beginning of the building of King Solomon's Temple, we should have the secrets of a Master Mason. I now demanded them." The other man spoke, "I cannot give them. Hiram, King of Tyre, and myself when we last met agreed that the secrets of a Master Mason should not be given until the completion of the Temple."

The first man spoke, "Behold, it is well nigh completed and I now demand the secrets of a Master Mason."

Again the man said, "I cannot give them."

"Then die," he said and marked a mark across my throat which was to indicate the cutting of an Entered Apprentice throat from ear to ear.

We went to the second station in very rapid movement. By this time I was totally confused, but knowing that all others before me had felt the same way, not truly believing that any bodily harm would come to me. Being taken very rapidly through this phase it worked on my mind. Coming to the second station, the same ceremonial situation transpired, except that my left breast was touched with a sharp instrument, which was to indicate the Fellow-Craft

Degree of having your left breast torn open.

Then I was led to the very front of the Lodge, and while still blindfolded, and not knowing what was happening, they began to rock me back and forth. Again the man spoke the same thing and those involved in the ceremony refused to give the word of a Master Mason. Unbeknown to me, a canvas was placed behind me, and as I was being rocked off balance, a huge cotton-filled leather mallet was used to strike me on the forehead, knocking me off my feet. (Later I would see men become violent at this point, others totally relaxed.) I gave a groan and hit the canvas. I was told to remain still, that they were not going to hurt me. All candidates are told the same.

When the acting out of the death of Hiram Abiff takes place the men gather around, enacting the workman of the temple, Fellow-Craft, Entered Apprentice, and Master Masons. They said, "Oh, what have we done? We've taken the life of our Grand Master, Hiram Abiff." Then they go through a ritual of taking you around the room as if you are being carried to a place and buried in the rubbish of the temple, then coming back and taking you out and carrying you to another place, which is to ceremoniously impress you that you are being buried. Then they go through the ceremony of trying to determine what happened to their Grand Master Hiram Abiff. Some were sent out to locate him. They bring in the three people who were supposedly the ones who had killed Hiram Abiff, or were involved in allowing it to be done. The guilty ones are taken outside the gates of the temple and executed. The rest come back and they begin to search where the body is buried. The ceremony continued as they find the grave, walk around singing a funeral dirge, while I lay there as a candidate.

They open the grave, (I was covered with the canvas in which they caught me), and the Master of the Lodge says, "Brother Junior Deacon, you will now raise the candidate by the **grip of an Entered Apprentice Mason**." He reaches down and pulls on my hand. Then he jerks his hand away and says, "Worshipful Master, the candidate cannot be raised by the grip of an Entered Apprentice Mason, because the skin slips from the flesh." Then they go through the ritual of the distress call, "Oh Lord, my God, is there no help for the widow's son," then he says, "You will now raise the body by the **grip of a Fellow-Craft Mason**." He grabbed my hand, but did not pull me up. He said, "Worshipful Master, the body cannot be raised by the grip of a Fellow-Craft Mason for the flesh cleaves from the bone."

"Let us pray," said the Worshipful Master. This is the prayer that is read over the body of a candidate as he enacts the death, burial, and resurrection of Hiram Abiff:

PRAYER

"Thou, 0 God, knowest our downsitting and our uprising, and understandest our thoughts afar off. Shield and defend us from the evil intentions of our enemies, and support us under the trials and affliction we are destined to endure while traveling through this vale of tears. Man that is born of a woman is of a few days and full of trouble. He cometh forth as a flower and is cut down; he fleeth also as a shadow, and continueth not. Seeing his days are determined, the number of his months are with Thee; Thou hast appointed his bonds that he cannot pass; turn from him that he may rest till he shall accomplish his day.

For there is hope of a tree, if it be cut down, that it will sprout again, and that the tender branch thereof will not cease. But man dieth and wasteth away; yea, man giveth up the ghost, and where is he? As the waters fail from the sea, and the flood decayeth and drieth up, so man lieth down and riseth not up to the heavens and shall be no more. Yet, 0 Lord! have compassion on the children of Thy creation; administer them comfort in time of trouble, and save them with an everlasting salvation! Amen." [12]

Much of the Scripture that is used in the Lodge is from the Old Testament, and is taken out of context and used very loosely. Scriptures are spoken only during the degrees and are read out of their manual. Never is the Word of God open to be read.

The Master then said, "My mind is now clear. The body shall be raised by the strong grip of the Lion's Paw of the tribe of Judah."

They grabbed me by the wrist and I theirs. Me being pulled up was to exemplify the resurrection of the body. As they pulled me up I was positioned hand to hand in the Master's grip, chest to chest, hand to back to show all three degree positions as one, then they spoke in my ear: "Maha-bone." **Maha-bone is the secret password of a Master Mason**.

That completed my Master Mason Degree, with the exception of being given a description of some of the work that had to be done, and reading to me the constitution and the by-laws of the Lodge, and some presentations. The following was the charge given me:

CHARGE

"My brother: Your zeal for the institution of Masonry, the progress you have made in the knowledge of its mysteries and your conformity to our regulations, have pointed you out as a proper object of our favor and esteem.

You are bound by duty, honor and gratitude, to be faithful to your trust; to support the dignity of your character on every occasion; and to enforce by precept and example, obedience to the tenets of the Order. In the character of a Master Mason, you are authorized to correct the irregularities of your less informed brethren, and guard them against a breach of fidelity. To preserve unsullied the reputation of the fraternity must be your constant care.

Universal benevolence, you are always to inculcate; and by the regularity of your own behavior, afford the best example for the conduct of others less informed.

The ancient *landmarks* of the order, entrusted to your care, you are carefully to preserve; and never suffer them to be infringed, or countenance a deviation from the established usages and customs of the fraternity.

Your virtue, honor and reputation, are concerned in supporting with dignity, the character you now bear. Let no motive, therefore, make you swerve from your duty, violate your vows, or betray your trust; but be true and faithful, and imitate the example of that celebrated artist you have this evening represented. Thus you will render yourself deserving of the honor which we have conferred, and merit the confidence you have reposed." [13]

The Lambskin

Next I was brought forward and presented with what is called the "Lambskin." This is the emblem of Free-masonry. These were the words spoken when it was presented:

ADDRESS TO A BROTHER UPON THE PRESENTATION OF A LAMBSKIN APRON BY THE LODGE *

"My brother, on behalf of this Lodge, I now present to you this white lambskin Apron. It may be, that in the coming years, upon your brow shall rest the laurel leaves of victory; it may be that, pendant from your breast, may hang jewels fit to grace the diadem of some Eastern potentate.

Aye! More than these, for light, added to coming light, may enable your ambitious feet to tread round after round of the ladder that leads to fame, in our Mystic Order; and even the purple of our fraternity may rest upon your honored shoulders; but never again, from mortal hands; never again, until your **enfranchised spirit shall have passed upward and inward, through the pearly gates,** can a greater honor be bestowed, or one more emblematical of purity and innocence, than that which has been conferred upon you tonight.

This Apron, the special gift of this Lodge, is yours to wear upon all proper occasions throughout an honorable life, and at your death, is to be placed upon the coffin that contains your lifeless remains and with them shall be laid beneath the silent clods of the valley.

May the pure and spotless surface of this Apron be an ever-present reminder of that "purity of heart and uprightness of conduct so essentially necessary", thus keeping pure your thoughts, and inspiring nobler deeds and greater achievements!

Then, when at last, your weary feet shall have come to the end of life's toilsome journey, and from your nerveless grasp, shall drop, forever, the working tools of life, may the record of your life and reactions be as pure and spotless as this Apron now is; and when your soul, freed from earth, shall stand naked and alone before the Great White Throne, may it be your portion to hear from Him Who sits thereon, the welcome plaudit: 'Well done, thou good and faithful servant! Enter thou into the joy of thy Lord!'"[14] (Emphasis mine)

Notice it says "never again from mortal hands, never again until your enfranchised spirit shall pass upward and inward through the pearly gates." Inferring that being a Mason, and doing what they say to do and living a good and righteous life will you get to heaven. Notice also the terms used, "him.. Of the tribe of Judah" and "Lambskin". What a mockery of our Lord and Savior Jesus, the True Lamb of God, the True Lion of the Tribe of Judah. The One who died for the sins of the world.

Christians know that the only way you are going to get into Heaven where God the Father resides, is through the blood of Jesus Christ.

Notice again the use of Scripture at the end: "Well done, thou good and faithful servant! Enter thou into the joy of thy Lord." Implying that your faithful service to the Lodge would be pleasing to the Lord Jesus. What mockery, what nonsense!

Once again congratulated by the others. I am now a full fledged Mason. Blind and in bondage, yet did not know it. God was setting the stage of life for my deliverance. **His pursuit will always result in His purpose!**

---

12 - L.M.L. pg. 79, 80
13 - L.M.L. pg. 92, 93
14 - L.M.L. pg. 93, 94

CHAPTER EIGHT

WORSHIPFUL MASTER

I wanted to be an officer, I wanted to be the Worshipful Master. I wanted all that I could get and endeavored to obtain it. After I turned my work into the lodge, I became very aggressive. I poured my heart into the work. I mowed the yard and helped landscape. I brought in new ideas because I was excited. I traveled anytime and anywhere to watch a degree be conferred. I was hungry to know all I could about Freemasonry.

One is not fully and openly accepted into the Masonic Lodge as a Master Mason until completion of all three degrees - the Entered Apprentice, the Fellow-Craft and the Master Mason. In all three degrees I spent many hours conversing back and forth with a man, while memorizing the Masonic work. I looked into and studied Mackey's Encyclopedia of Freemasonry. I asked questions of the brethren.

They taught me the historical work involved in putting on the degrees and learning how to function in the stations within the Masonic Lodge.

I pursued further recognition in the lodge by joining the "Scottish Rite". I became a 32nd degree Scottish Rite Mason.

This degree, like other advanced degrees are purchased. After paying a yearly fee (dues) you are required to sit through a day long drama concerning the degree you have chosen, whether it be the Scottish Rite, Shrine, or whatever. No memory work is required.

All the above degrees are status degrees. The degree of Master Mason and position of Worshipful Master is the highest that can be obtained.

As I began my journey deeper into Masonry, God had another idea. We lived in Alief, Texas at the time. God was convicting me to cut back on the Freemasonry work and to yield to Him. At first I didn't recognize it as being the Spirit of God, but thought of it as trying to get my life in order and make something of it. I don't recall anyone walking up to me on the street and witnessing to me about Jesus. None of my relatives asked, "Do you know Jesus loves you?" No one told me I was on the road to destruction. One doesn't have to go around telling people how bad they are, they already know it. We are to tell people that Jesus loves them and that there is a better life. No one witnessed to me. The Holy Spirit of God began to woo me back in such a dramatic way. I had gone in and I had gone out of His loving embrace. Though I had left Him, He never forsook me. I knew that my life was out of order. Everything I had was crumbling, yet I was holding on with everything that I had. It is the thief who comes to steal, kill and destroy. But Jesus said, *"...I am come that they might have life, and that they might have it more abundantly."* (John 10:10)

I progressed very rapidly through the ranks of Freemasonry, learning how to open and close the Lodge in every degree and station. That meant I could take any position in the Lodge, fill in, and do it properly and very proficiently. I learned how to confer every degree in every station, with the exception of the Master's Degree, but was very close to being proficient in that. This is actually a tremendous accomplishment. I could quote Masonic work nonstop from memory for a long time, yet I didn't know three verses of Scripture - and claimed to be a Christian.

I traveled all over the Houston area and the Southern part of Texas to be involved in Lodge meetings and conferring of degrees, but I wouldn't go to church right down the street from my house. Many Masons substitute the goodness and supposed godliness of the Lodge for the coming together of believers and the teaching of the Bible. **It was a form**

of godliness but it was not God!

One night on the way to a Lodge meeting a thought invaded my mind. As I passed three churches and pulled into the Lodge driveway this thought came very strongly, **"Isn't it something how I will go to Lodge meeting faithfully? Isn't it something how I go to every one of these meetings and drive right by the doors of a church but never go in?"**

I never missed a meeting in the years that I was involved in Masonry, but what I was doing wasn't satisfactory to the Lord. What was happening in my life was that God wanted to purge my conscience from the dead works that I was doing in the Lodge. I knew I had to get right with Him. But by this time I was what is called the Senior Warden, which is one step from being the Master of the Lodge. God had been dealing with me for three years. I was in my fourth year of Masonry and was rapidly approaching the time that I would obtain the position as head man - or better known among the Masons as the Worshipful Master of Sugar Land Lodge #1141.

I was still searching for light. But the hoodwink was about to be removed. The Holy Spirit had been setting the stage to penetrate the darkness of the Masonic Order. **The true light of Jesus Christ was about to explode on the scene.**

CHAPTER NINE

FOLLOW ME

My wife and I had been taking our children to Sunday school because we knew they needed to be in church. Isn't it amazing how we justify our lifestyles all the while demanding better for others. "Do as I say - not as I do!" At this time I still kept my business open seven days a week. I yielded to the Spirit of God and said to Tena, "We need to get involved in a church. Would you go with me, back to the church that I was brought up in?" I felt impressed to go back to the First Baptist Church of Stafford where I had first met the Lord.

We went back. I'm thoroughly convinced that once you begin to fellowship with believers you cannot sit under the Word of God without yielding your life to the Lord - unless you are only playing church. The Lord began to convict me more and more and more.

One Sunday at church as I sat with my family, the Spirit of God spoke to me and said, (not audibly, but in my spirit) "You have a choice to make; come and follow Me or reject Me. If you reject Me, hell awaits you, if you follow me, Heaven awaits. I got out of the pew and walked to the front of the church and cried so much that the pastor had no idea what was happening. But he knew that God was doing a work in my life, and the sin in my life was being lifted. God knew my heart. We don't have to stand before men and proclaim what we've done, our actions speak for us. I gave my heart to Jesus, and as I wept and wept I heard footsteps in the back ground. It was Tena. She had a Catholic background, but never knew Jesus. That day we made a committed decision. "No turning back - ever!" As a Baptist we were taught to rededicate our life. I am not speaking against that principle of the church. But as for me, I had, as a young person rededicated my life so many times that I often have said, "My dedicator broke." Now we made a commitment, no matter what, we would forever follow Jesus.

We men, look at our homes and wonder why they are not in order. We look at our wives and children and demand change in them when all the while we need to get ourselves right. It begins with the man of the house. We need to put things in their right order!

God's divine plan is for the man to be the king and priest of his home. Not to lord over it, but lead it with loving care. The wife and children will lovingly stand with him, supporting him. Divine order brings Divine flow which produces Divine peace.

Tena came forward and gave her heart to Jesus. My two sons and daughter gave their hearts to Jesus. My family was made whole.

Instantly God delivered me from much of the lust of the flesh where I had been involved in every filthy thing that was available. He instantly delivered me from the filthiness of my mouth by cleaning up my speech. **From the altar of prayer and commitment I went home and cleaned up my house. I cleaned out my place of business**. The filthy literature was removed. Things that I kept in my home and business that were displeasing to the Lord were removed. I was still drinking, the Lord was yet to deal with me very severely about that. Sin had to be purged from my life.

I was still involved in the rituals of performing my duties at the Lodge and God was convicting me. He dealt with me about closing my business on Sunday. I knew there was a calling on my life to devote more and more of my time to the Lord. I gave Him more and more of me. He wanted me completely, but, you know, God won't make you do anything, He wants you to come to Him freely. *"....Freely ye have received, freely give."* (Mathew 10:8) I wanted to give all I had to the Lord. There were things that were still in my life that were not pleasing to Him. I took time to listen to the Word of God and to study it. As I read the Word of God I saw that God wanted all of me.

Now I was turning my efforts, my physical labor toward the church. The things that I was doing for the Lodge, I began to do for Jesus. I'd mow the yard, clean the church, just offer my physical labor in any possible way that I could help. I wanted to do things for Jesus. I wanted to produce fruit. The Word of God was permeating my soul. It came into my spirit. It began to come alive in my life.

I knew I had to close my store on Sunday, and I was warring with the Lord.

At that point I wasn't trusting God for everything. I knew that He wanted my life. I didn't understand about trusting God, although my pastor preached on how we need to turn things over to the Lord, and how He cares about our financial areas - every area of our life. God was dealing with me to close my store on Sunday and I would argue with the Spirit of the Lord. I would not close - I could not close. The money I was making was going for bills and I had to have it. It was absolutely necessary because I had extended myself to the very limit. Every dime I brought in was essential to just exist.

One night my pastor preached about God wanting to

take control of everything we have. I went forward and said, "God's telling me to close my store and I won't close it; pray with me." We prayed and I asked the Lord to lead me and direct me in seeking His guidance.

When you ask God for something, you go to His Word and find the Scripture that fits the situation and obey it.. I read in James 1:5-8: *"If any lack wisdom, let him ask of God, that giveth to all men liberally, and upbraideth not; and it shall be given him. But let him ask in faith, nothing wavering. For he that wavereth is like a wave of the sea driven with the wind and tossed. For let not that man think that he shall receive anything of the Lord. A double-minded man is unstable in all his ways."*

I stood on this verse because I needed wisdom. But if you are changing your prayer and changing your mind, and you are not sure what you really want, then you haven't made up your mind. The Word of God says that you'll not receive anything from the Lord, because a double-minded man is unstable in all his ways. My mind was open, I dared to ask God for wisdom.

A few days later my oldest son, who was thirteen years old, came to me because he heard his mother and me sharing about wanting to close on Sunday but not knowing how. The Spirit of God used him.

He told me that he would give up his allowance, his bicycle and other things if Daddy would just close on Sunday and come and be home with the family.

My heart broke. I went to church again, talked to a friend which owned a plumbing business. I told him I really did not understand the Word of God that much, but I found a scripture that fit my situation. Matthew 18: 19, *"Again, I say unto you, That if two of you shall agree on earth as touching any thing that they shall ask, it shall be done for them of my Father which is in heaven."*

I told him I had discovered Hebrews 11: 6, *"But without faith it is impossible to please him; for he that cometh to God must believe that he is, and that he is a rewarder of them that diligently seek him."* I said, if I am truly going to trust God, then I had to put actions with my faith, because I had also read James 1: 22, *"But be ye doers of the word, and not hearers only, deceiving your own selves."* and James 2: 20, *"But wilt thou know, O vain man, that faith without works is dead?"*

I will never forget what he said. "Richard, you had better be careful, you don't won't to go broke." Wow! Just what I needed. Doubt and unbelief.

In spite of his doubt and unbelief he was still willing to agree with me and I was ready to agree with God's Word.

As we prayed a great peace came upon me, I knew somehow everything would be alright.

Monday morning I went to the store. I told my manager we'd never open on Sunday again as long as I lived. He looked at me like I had lost my mind. He knew how much money we were taking in and everything about the business. I took a hammer and beat off every sign on the building that read: Open on Sundays. I said, **"Lord, it's yours."** That day my business increased to the point that it more than met what I was doing on Sunday. I never reopened the doors on Sunday, and I knew that God was truly in my life.

I told those who worked for me that I had been responsible for them not being able to go to church. Now their excuse was removed. I encouraged them to follow the Lord. They were a witness to my life, before and during my encounter. My life spoke for itself. They knew God was working overtime in my life.

Those who I led into darkness through my lifestyle of sin were now being affected by "God's invasion". Later I had the privilege of leading each one to Jesus and His saving grace.

I saw the blessings of Jesus. God was coming alive in my life. I began to look to the Word and to study it, knowing something more was available to me. Jesus said with signs and wonders He'll confirm His Word. *"And they went forth, and preached every where, the Lord working with them, and confirming the word with signs following."* (Mark 16:20) Again the Lord dealt with me about another area in my life: I still had alcohol in our home. Oh, I had quit going to the beer joints, but on Friday and Saturday evenings I was a six-pack King. I would drink my six-pack. Every time I drank it might as well have been a 55-gallon drum of beer because I could hardly get one beer down. I wanted it, my flesh was craving alcohol. Again, I would not yield to the Spirit of God. I would answer people who asked me, "What do you think about drinking?" I would reply with: "As long as you don't get drunk, it doesn't hurt." It made my conscience feel good to water down the Word. That was a deception from the forces of darkness. It does hurt because there's no good thing that comes from consuming alcohol, nothing but heartache.

Again I wouldn't yield to the Lord. He pressed me very heavily. Alcohol was one of the last areas in my life that needed to be gone. It was like a huge mountain. The Bible says that we are to say unto that mountain be thou removed and cast into the sea and it has to go in the name of Jesus. (Mark 11:23)

Again the Lord was about to use my oldest son. All

through my young adult married life I drank and my children watched me. I was teaching my children how to drink by example. They used to go into some of the beer joints with me. They've seen me fight. They saw the pure hell that this earth had to offer. They watched their daddy and thought it was alright because Daddy did it. Children watch every move the parent makes. As you do the works of the devil they'll copy that. Then when you teach them that Jesus Christ is inside of you, and that you are doing the work of Jesus, and that you are going about doing the works that the Lord has created you to do, they will follow you.

My son went down the street to a neighbor's house and got drunk. When he came home and I saw him, my first thought was: Oh Lord, drugs! Then I recognized that he was drunk. My temper flared and I grabbed him and carried him to his room. He fell back on his bed and as he bounced up, I grabbed him and cried out: "Oh God, help me; I love him, I don't want to hurt him." Jeremiah 33:3 says, *"Call unto me, and I will answer thee, and shew thee great and mighty things, which thou knowest not."* When I called on the name of God the Father, Jesus bathed me in love. All I could do was to hold my son and cry. I cried, he cried, and his mother cried. Then we went to the living room and sat down. All I wanted to do was to hug and love him because I had been bathed in supernatural love for him.

The Spirit of God came upon me and spoke Scripture to me. The Lord often speaks with His Word. The Spirit spoke to me out of Galatians 6:7-8 *"Be not deceived; God is not mocked: for whatsoever a man soweth, that shall he also reap. For he that soweth to his flesh shall of the flesh reap corruption; but he that soweth to the Spirit shall of the Spirit reap life everlasting."* I knew exactly what the Lord meant. That got into my spirit so deep because I had shown my children the filthiness of the world, how to fight and how to drink, and I was reaping what I had sown. I confessed to my family that I had been wrong and asked them to forgive me.

That night I went into my cabinets and into the refrigerator and poured all my alcohol down the sink. I swore before the Lord that I'd never touch it to my lips again as long as I lived. God took that out of my life only because I gave it to Him. The desire for alcohol would rise in me and I had to go back to the Word where it says in Matthew 18:19 about two or more of us agreeing. I agreed with a Christian brother one night and said, "Brother, just agree with me that I won't yield to this thing and that the Lord will take away the desire." He prayed in total agreement, and the desire to drink left and never returned.

Now the Lord was so involved in my life that I could not resist His call. I knew that there was something different about my pastor. I noticed he had joy that I didn't have. I said, "Lord, I've given you everything. I've given you my family, my business, and all the things that were in my life, yet I don't have the fullness and the happiness that I need. I want to know what is missing."

He answered: "ASK YOUR PASTOR."

I talked to my pastor and kept watching his life. He shared about the baptism of the Holy Spirit. I wasn't too sure that this "baptism" was of God. I knew it was in the Bible, but I had been taught that you just didn't do those kind of things, it had passed away.

As I kept watching my pastor I'd tell my wife, "He's fixin' to dance in the church." We were still a Southern Baptist Church, and boy, people were getting stirred up about him. I'd look at him and say, "He's going to speak in tongues, and when he does, we're getting out of here."

The pastor invited Tena and I to go to a meeting of Charles and Frances Hunter, well-known charismatic leaders. We went to the meeting with three or four other people, along with the pastor. As we sat there the music began. There was such peace and joy there! Then the music stopped and the people praised God and sang in what they called "the Spirit." At the time I didn't know what it was, but it sounded like angels singing. It was the most beautiful thing I had ever experienced. I heard my pastor praising God in another language. I knew it was godly, but I didn't understand it.

We sat through the whole meeting watching the mighty moving of the Holy Spirit; people were delivered instantly of the cigarette habit, giving their hearts to the Lord and receiving the baptism of the Holy Spirit, with the evidence of speaking in other tongues. I was totally consumed by it, but did not yield.

On the way out going home, I bought a book by Charles and Frances Hunter, **Why Should I Speak in Tongues?** I got in the car and threw the book on the dashboard. "What in the world did I buy that trash for?" I asked. My old doctrine was coming out of me. I threw it on the dash, but I didn't throw it out of the window. That night I read three or four pages of the book and said, "Man, I don't know why I bought this book," and tossed it on the table.

Every day when I came home from work I would threaten to throw the book in the trash, but the more I read, the more I knew that I wanted what I was reading. I read of the tremendous testimonies of the life-changing experiences of the baptism of the Holy Spirit. It described what Joel 2:28-29 says: *"And it shall come to pass afterward, that I will pour out my spirit upon all flesh; and your sons and your daugh-*

ters shall prophesy, your old men shall dream dreams, your young men shall see visions: and also upon the servants and upon the handmaids in those days will I pour out my spirit."

I called my pastor and said, "You've got to come to the house."

He came and brought the Word of God with him. I said, "You show me in the Word of God where the baptism of the Holy Spirit is of God and for today." The very thing I tried to disprove, God showed me. I had such a hunger in my heart that I couldn't sit still, yet I would not yield.

Later I went to a Full Gospel Businessmen's Meeting at the Shamrock Hilton Hotel. The speaker called for those who wanted to receive the baptism of the Holy Spirit. I ran down the aisle. I threw up my hands. A man came along and touched me and I began to speak in other tongues. The Bible says that anything we do without love is as a tinkling symbol and sounding brass. To me the greatest evidence was not the tongues but the love in my heart. I had a love for people that I once hated. God was purging my life and preparing me for service with power and zeal.

I left the hotel on a high. Higher than any drug or alcohol could ever give me. I had turned into a different man. I drove straight to one of my best friend's shops. He was a wood worker and lived in his shop. I just had to tell someone what great things the Lord was doing. He was it!

When I arrived he was drinking beer and working. I said, "Dan sit down, I've got to tell you something." He sat down on a box with his beer. For the next two hours I shared everything I knew. He looked at me and said, "Something has surely happened, you're as high as a kite." He did not accept Jesus that day, but later God graciously saved him and he built a beautiful pulpit in the form of the cross which is still being used today. God is awesome!

CHAPTER TEN

COME OUT

Our church had a tent revival. A number of preachers and teachers were brought in to minister. All were great men of God. Lester Roloff was one, and Dr. John R. Rice another. I subscribed to a little paper called, "The Sword of the Lord" by Dr. Rice's ministry. There was an article in that paper about Masonry and how men had come out of the BONDAGE OF MASONRY through a book that Dr. Rice had written. I thought to myself, Who does he think he is? But I sent for the book, **Lodges Examined by the Bible**. When I received the baptism of the Holy Spirit, the truth of the Word began to come alive in me. As I read the book, it changed my life.

I went to the men in the Lodge and asked them, "What about the obligations that we took?"

"It is only ceremonial; it has no meaning," those who answered said.

My response to them was, "If the obligation has no meaning what are we doing in Masonry, what are we doing placing our hand on the Bible to take the vow?"

As I asked those and other questions, I noticed a stirring in my spirit. After I read the whole book, the Holy Spirit revealed to me that I needed to **COME OUT OF MASONRY**. It was at the time to be inducted as the Worshipful Master of Sugar Land Lodge #1141, a height of achievement that I had sought to obtain since I entered Masonry. Would God require me to come out from among them now?

I said, "Oh, Lord, I must stay in, these men are depending on me."

The date was April 1976. I was installed as the Worshipful Master for the year of service from 1976 - 1977.

I went under the pretense of doing God's work. Each petition for a candidate of the Lodge had to come before me. I would witness to them and ask them if they knew Jesus. God honored that, but it was not His best for me. It did cause a lot of stirring among the Masonic brethren.

I instituted some good works by passing a resolution that for each member, we would donate money to be given into our local community once a year. We had about 140 members, and that wasn't a big thing but it was at least a step. We had never done any works such as that in the area. I helped to pass resolutions that money would be given out once a year regardless of race, or religion. I knew it was a selfish organization and I was trying in my own strength to change things. I told them that our walls were closed off and the works of the Lodge were not made known to anybody in our community.

I served that year but I was a miserable man, because I was disobedient to the Spirit of God. When I finished my last scheduled meeting of Sugar Land Lodge, I came home and once again the Lord said, "Get out."

A man has no way out of the Masonic Lodge after he realizes what he has entered. They do not leave you a way out that you can honorably walk away from and no longer be associated. You may disassociate yourself from the local Lodge, but you are always a member of the Grand Lodge of your State until they see fit to excommunicate, expel or suspend you.

I wrote a letter to my local Lodge and told them I had given my heart and my life to Jesus Christ and that I would demit from the Lodge - which simply put me in a state of nonexistence in the local body yet still a member of the Grand Lodge of Texas.

CHAPTER ELEVEN

FATHERHOOD
OF GOD

During my last year in Masonry I studied different aspects of the Order. Masons will tell you that it is not a religion, but I pray as you read and study what is revealed to you, that you will see that it is so **interwoven with religion** it causes a person to subconsciously submit to its form of religion. Even the **Masonic Manual states that Masonry is a religion** - much to the surprise of many Masons.

"The Religious Doctrines of Masonry are very simple and self-evident; they are designated by no perplexities of sectarian theology, but stand out in the broad light, intelligible and acceptable by all minds having a belief in God, and in the Immortality of the Soul. He who denies these tenets can be no Mason, for the RELIGIOUS DOCTRINES of the Institution significantly embrace them in every part of its ritual. The Neophyte no sooner crosses the threshold of the Lodge than he is called upon to recognize, as a first duty, an entire trust in the superintending care and love of the Supreme Being, and the Ceremonies of

Initiation into Symbolic Masonry terminate by revealing the symbol of a life after death, and an entrance upon Immortality. Now this and the former class of doctrines are intimately connected and mutually dependent, for we must first know and feel the universal Fatherhood of God, before we can rightly appreciate the universal Brotherhood of Man. The Old Charges prescribe that a Mason, while left to his particular opinions, must be of that "religion in which all men agree; that is to say, the religion which teaches the existence of God and an eternal life."[15] (Emphasis mine)

As you have just seen, Masonry declares that it is a religion. It is **A RELIGION WITHOUT JESUS**, a religion of morality.

THE MORAL LAW

"A Mason", say the old charges, "is obliged by his tenure to obey the *Moral law*." Since it is, by ancient custom and usage, the duty and obligation of every Mason to obey the Moral law, these Commentaries would be deficient without a brief consideration of that important subject.

Morality seems to be the first outward manifestation of Masonic philosophy. It is a prime prerequisite for admission into the rites of initiation. Masonry is described as a "beautiful *system of Morality* veiled in allegories and illustrated by symbols."

A careful investigation of this important subject will reveal the fact that Moral preparation is an essential necessity before the Neophite can actually enter upon the *path* of true initiation.

The Moral law is the gateway through which one enters the straight and narrow pathway that leads to spiritual awakening and unfoldment, which may be said to be the ultimate object to be accomplished by the rites of initiation.

No one who reads the ancient charges can fail to see that Freemasonry is a strictly moral Institution, and that the principles it inculcates inevitably tend to make a brother who obeys its precepts a more honorable and virtuous man. Hence, the lectures very properly define Freemasonry to be "a science of Morality"......" [16]

MASONRY IS TRULY A RELIGION OF MORALITY AND GOOD WORKS, A RELIGION WITHOUT CHRIST AND THE BLOOD THAT WAS SHED FOR YOU AND I FOR THE REMISSION OF SINS. SALVATION THROUGH CHRIST IS A GIFT OF GOD AND NOT OF WORKS.

Many men, women and young adults that love God

and worship Jesus have been seduced into LEAVING THE FAITH and have begun to put their faith and labors into the Masonic Lodge and its different branches. They will not receive anything that is contrary to what the Masonic Lodge has burned into their minds. Their conscience has been seared with a hot iron, therefore they have turned their minds and hearts away from what the Holy Spirit is teaching and asking them to follow. They are totally relying upon the Lodge for their need to be in fellowship.

Masonry is also interwoven with much of the ancient customs of heathen cultures, such as the study of the zodiac and the signs and symbols surrounding it. This is absolutely forbidden by God. Many ancient Egyptian cult symbols and ceremonies are used in the rites of Initiation, along with many other ancient ceremonies, such as the Muhammadans, Hindus, and the Druids used, which are all forbidden by God to be used or practiced in any way. MASONRY IS IN FACT A TOOL OF SATAN TO DECEIVE THE WORLD. *"Now the Spirit speaketh expressly, that in the latter times some shall depart from the faith, giving heed to seducing spirits, and doctrines of devils; speaking lies in hypocrisy; having their conscience seared with a hot iron."* (1 Timothy 4:1-2)

The day will come that the works of the Masonic Lodge will be brought forth before God Himself, and the Lord will speak. *"Many will say to me in that day, Lord, Lord, have we not prophesied in thy name? and in thy name have cast out devils? and in thy name done many wonderful works?"* (Matthew 7:22) **GOOD WORKS WILL NOT GET YOU TO HEAVEN**. You need to have spiritual fruit following your life. You need to produce good fruit, but it must be produced through Jesus. No other way will be recognized. Jesus then said in Matthew 7:23-27: *"And then will I profess unto them, I never knew you: depart from me, ye that work iniquity. Therefore, whosoever heareth these sayings of mine, and doeth them, I will liken him unto a wise man, which built his house upon a rock: And the rain descended, and the floods came, and the winds blew, and beat upon that house; and it fell not: for it was founded upon a rock. And every one that heareth these sayings of mine, and doeth them not, shall be likened unto a foolish man, which built his house upon the sand: And the rain descended, and the floods came, and the winds blew, and beat upon that house; and it fell: and great was the fall of it."*

The works of the Masonic Lodge are built on a sandy foundation, and the winds and the rain shall wash it out from under it, and it shall crumble because it is not built upon the rock, which is Jesus Christ.

---

15 - L.M.L. pg. 239, 240

16 - L.M.L. pg. 287, 288

CHAPTER TWELVE

THE DEVIL'S DESIGN

From the history of early America, Masonry has been woven into our nation. George Washington, who was a practicing Mason was inspirational in placing Masonic symbols in our nations capital. Should we say George Washington designed Masonry into our nation? No! It's **THE DEVIL'S DESIGN**. The works of the devil to bring a people under a curse.

Look closely at the Washington Monument. What do you see? A monument to our first president? No! Although Congress had originally requested a statue of George Washington on a horse, what they got was a 555 foot tall, 55 foot wide obelisk. An emblem representing the procreative power of the Egyptian sun-god. It's **THE DEVIL'S DESIGN**. Much of Masonry has its roots in ancient Egyptian cult worship. The compass and square emblems most often noted for Masonry, represents ancient solar deities.

Albert Pike, grand commander of Scottish Rite Freemasonry in the last 1800's, taught that the square and compass, along with the Bible, were "the great lights of Freemasonry". He accomplished the most dangerous of mixtures. True faith with pagan deities.

The god of Masonry is a god everyone but a discerning Christian can be comfortable with. Albert Pike greatly influenced and promoted **"The Devil's Design"**.

The publication **Angel of Light** (available from Chic Publications, P.O. Box 662, Chino, California 91710), exposes scripturally how Satan has formed many occult organizations throughout the world. On page 30 of this book is a paragraph which exposes Albert Pike as having proclaimed before an assembly of Scottish Rite Inspectors General that **lucifer is God**:

"Albert Pike (Sovereign Pontiff of Universal Freemasonry) said, "That which we must say to the crowd is: We worship a god, but it is the god that one adores without superstition." "To you Sovereign Grand Inspectors General, we say this, that you may repeat it to the brethren of the 32nd, 31st and 30th degrees - the MASONIC RELIGION should be by all of us initiates of the high degrees, maintained in the purity of the Luciferian Doctrine." "If lucifer were not God, would Adonay (Jesus... God of the Christians)... calumniate him (bother to spread false and harmful statements about him)?" **"Yes, lucifer is God..."**[17] (Emphasis mine)

(This statement was originally taken from the publication "Occult Theocracy" by Lady Queensborough, pgs. 220-221; published by Emissary Publications, P.O. Box 642, South Pasadena, California 91031).

THE DEVIL'S DESIGN?

To infiltrate a society in any and every way possible. To deceive, to delute, to destroy the pure faith and worship of God.

What can we do? Sound the alarm, cry out to the people. *"Do not be unequally yoked with unbelievers (do not make mismated alliances with them or come under a different yoke with them, inconsistent with your faith). For what partnership have right living and right standing with God with iniquity and lawlessness? Or how can light have fellowship with darkness? What harmony can there be between Christ and Belial (the devil)? Or what has a believer in common with an unbeliever? What agreement (can there be between) a temple of God and idols? For we are the temple of the living God; even as God said, I will dwell in and with and among them and will walk in and with and among them, and I will be their God, and they shall be My people."* II Corinthians 6: 14-18, (Amplified Bible - Zondervan Bible Publishers).

---

17 - C. P.

CHAPTER THIRTEEN

THE CALL

Our pastor resigned from the church, and I was thrust into a faith walk. There was an interim period without a pastor at the church. As a Trustee of the church, I transacted most of the business of the church and saw to it that it ran properly as an administrator, and also did some teaching and preaching for some of the services.

A new Pastor was sent by the Lord to pastor the church. I continued to grow in the understanding of the Word as the anointing on my life increased.

Many men came to me for recommendation and to sign their petition to become a Lodge member. I never solicited anyone - the men came to me. God sent people that He wanted me to minister to. I shared with those He sent about what God was doing in my life and how He had called me out of the Lodge. I gave them a copy of the book by Dr. John R. Rice. **Lodges Examined by the Bible**, (Dr. John R. Rice, Sword of the Lord Publications, Box 1099, Murfreesboro, Tennessee 37130).

God had placed a calling on my life and I knew it. The beautiful part about God's calling on a man's life is that He'll also call his wife. Look at a successful ministry and you'll see that when God calls a man, He also calls the wife. God never destroys or separates a home where husband and wife are concerned. God brings it together in all the purity that it was intended to be. God called my wife and me to a work, we were teaching and ministering the Word together.

Unaware that anything was transpiring at Sugar Land Lodge, I continued my walk in the ministry of the Lord. A member of the Lodge had complained about me handing out Dr. Rice's book and had filed a formal complaint.

December 29, 1978, a deputy sheriff of the Fort Bend County Sheriff's Department, who was also a member of the Sugar Land Lodge, entered my store and said, "I have a summons for you."

Instantly I thought, Now what in the world is going on? I connected it with the criminal laws of Texas.

The deputy remarked, "I'm not here representing the State of Texas: I'm here representing the Lodge."

We went into my office. He handed me the summons which read: "Summons to the accused, to

Brother Richard Frank Ford: You're hereby notified that the Worshipful Master of this Lodge has appointed the hour of ten o'clock a.m. on the 17th day of February, 1979, as a time in the hall of Sugar Land Lodge as a place for the trial of the charges filed against you in this Lodge on the 21st day of June 1978 and you're hereby cited to appear at said time and place to make your defense thereof."

The deputy also handed me the charges. It said that I influenced two Entered Apprentices to not pursue completing their degree by presenting them a book to read which contradicted Masonry and represented it as being against the Bible, quoting violating article #506, paragraph 2, 9, 10, and article #505 of the Grand Lodge of Texas, which simply states that I was doing things that were unbecoming of a Master Mason.

I became angry and said, "I won't honor this and you can take it and do what you want to with it."

"Well, it doesn't make any difference to me," said the deputy, "because whether you come or not, we'll have the trial. It is your prerogative whether you want to come or not."

"I will not honor it. I'll have no part of it. You need to leave and leave me alone," I answered, but the Spirit of God spoke to me: "Yes, you'll go."

I hesitated and then questioned, "Lord?"

Again He said, "Yes, you will go."

Peace settled over me and I looked at the deputy and said, "Yes, I will go. I will see you on February 17th at ten o'clock, at the Lodge, for the Masonic trial.

The Spirit of God impressed me to go into my closet and look on the top shelf. There was my briefcase with my apron, and many mementos of the Masonic Lodge as well as several books on the Lodge.

The Lord said, "Destroy the mementos and apron, keep the books".

At the time I didn't know why, I was to keep the Lightfoot's Manual of the Lodge, and the Rules and By-Laws, and Constitution and Resolution of the Grand Lodge of Texas, but God knew I would later use them in the research and writing of this book, as well as preparation for what was yet before me. Everything else I put in the garbage compactor and mashed the button, rings, jewelry and everything. **I broke all bondages and ties with the organization.**

I would like to tell you that it was a simple thing to do, but it was not. The spirit of fear and seed of bondage had taken deep roots, **strongholds had developed**.

The subtlety of the devil is to produce thoughts that will entice us to stop and consider and then act upon the thoughts he has planted. Everything begins with a thought. Then we progress to imagination which when pondered upon will produce actions, which when acted upon will produce bondages which in turn produces strongholds. (II Corinthians 10: 3-6)

I allowed my inquisitiveness to pull me into a forbidden zone, my lack of knowledge in God's Word would be my downfall. Once I began to think on the Masonic Lodge, I moved to seeing myself involved, which produced an action on my part, which opened the door to bondage and strongholds.

Over a period of several weeks, God continued to move on me to destroy all ties with the organization. Having stopped my involvement and renouncing the organization was not enough. God was showing me how powerful and deeply rooted the bondage was. Yet, God is greater!

When I broke through and destroyed the symbols of Masonry, a peace filled my soul greater than I could ever had imagined.

I thought I had been released from Masonry but now I was truly SET FREE.

Four months later I was faced with a Masonic trial.

I got the books on Masonry and began to study them. I especially read the law books of the Lodge. The Lord said, "This is what you will do." He gave me the ideas and I wrote them down. I wanted to go to the Lodge and do what I wanted to do, but the Lord would not let me. I had to do things God's way.

I dreaded going to the trial. It was a very hard thing for me to do. In fact, it is never easy when the enemy rises up against you. When the devil sets himself to war against us he uses fear and intimidation. David when facing the giant Goliath was hit with both of these spirits of the enemy. Goliath a nine foot giant, a voice roaring threats, proclaiming victory over a seemingly weaker opponent. Yet it seems that the devil never learns, one thing he keeps forgetting, **THE ANOINTING.**

I felt like David, fear and intimidation was ministering to me. But God was releasing the anointing. The power that causes His enemies to tremble. As I prepared myself to go, I sought prayer support from others. They earnestly prayed for me. (James 5:16) I realized that all of the things that I had gone through, like serving in the church during the period of time when we were without a pastor, helped build my faith, as well as other encounters. At that time faith was at a point that I could believe God for anything - God had prepared me.

Approximately fifty members of the church came to the Lodge Hall. It was a day of history for the Lodge, the church and me. For the Lodge, because they had never had a Master Mason put on trial in all of its fifty year history. Never had their Worshipful Master walked away and denied the Lodge.

The church had never gone against any Masonic Lodge. Most churches believe that Lodges are good. As I was in the building going through the trial, the people of the church were marching around the Lodge singing praises to God, lifting their hands like the children of God when they marched around the walls of Jericho. Some were so thoroughly convinced that the walls of the Lodge would crumble they would not get too close to the building.

I often wondered, "Did they think about me. If the walls did fall, what about me? Hey, I am inside." I laugh about it every time I think about it.

The Lord showed me that there would be weeping and gnashing of teeth in the Lodge that day, and that many men would leave because of what I did. Many would lay down their jewels of the Masonic Order and walk away and never touch them again. Not everyone would do what I did, submitting to a trial.

The night before I went to the Lodge, I had one strong urge in my heart. The same urge was there the next morning. It was to run because the enemy was trying to defeat me. Satan told me I would lose all my business, and that those men would come against me and destroy everything I had.

SUMMONS TO ACCUSED

To Brother _Richard Frank Ford_

You are hereby notified that the Worshipful Master of this Lodge has appointed the hour of _10:00_ o'clock _A._ M., on the _17th_ day of _February_, 19_78_, as the time, and the Hall of _Sugar Land Lodge_ as the place, for the trial of the charges filed against you in this Lodge on the _21st_ day of _June_, 19_78_, and you are hereby cited to appear at said time and place to make your defense thereto.

A copy of the charges and specifications is hereto attached.

Witness my hand and the seal of _Sugar Land_ Lodge No. _1141_ this the _19th_ day of _December_, 19 78.

(Seal)

Andrew J Blair, Secretary.

MASONIC HOME PRESS

CERTIFICATE OF SERVICE

I hereby certify that on the 29 day of DECEMBER, 19 78, at STAFFORD,

State of TEXAS, I served the foregoing citation and copy of charges and specifications therein

referred to upon RICHARD FRANK FORD, therein named,

(a) By delivering a copy thereof to said RICHARD FRANK FORD personally;

(b) By depositing in a United States postoffice at _____ State of Texas, a copy of said citation, together with a certified copy of said charges and specifications, in a sealed envelope, the letter duly registered, and the address of the said _____ properly written thereon, and upon which envelope was endorsed an order to the postmaster to return the same to the Secretary of this Lodge if not delivered within ten days. Said letter was addressed to the last known address of said _____ _____, his usual place of abode being unknown to the undersigned, after due and diligent search to discover same;

(c) I have been unable, after due and diligent search and effort to find the abode of accused, or any information relative to his whereabouts. (Here state any other facts, such as accused secreting himself, being a fugitive from justice, or any fact showing why he cannot be found. If he cannot be found, and his last known address is secured, then make certificate as provided under (b) above.)

....

....

Dated this 29 TH day of DECEMBER, 19 78.

....

Tiler (or Member) of SUGAR LAND Lodge No. 1411

NOTE: The Tiler or member serving the summons will use the form (a), (b), or (c), according to the manner of service and omit the other paragraphs so marked.

Form No. 4. Copyrighted. 6-58-1M.

134

CHARGES

To the Worshipful Master, Wardens and Brethren of _____ SUGAR LAND _____

Lodge No. ____1141_____, A. F. & A. M.:

I hereby charge Brother____RICHARD FRANK FORD_____, ~~a member of this~~

~~Lodge, No. _____~~ _____ ~~Lodge No.~~ _____ ,~~or~~ a non-affiliated Mason residing within the jurisdiction of this Lodge, as the case may be) with un-Masonic conduct, to-wit:

Specification 1: In that the said Brother___Ford_____
Prior to the
on or about the _____19th____day of ____December_____, 1977_, at Stafford, Texas___, did

(Here described in plain and concise language the facts constituting the offense, which must be charged with certainty, and the time, place, and all particulars distinctly specified. A general charge of un-Masonic conduct without specifications shall not be entertained. If charges involve matter not properly written, it should be so stated, and the accused, at the time of arraignment, should be orally informed of the specific facts, to which the trial must then be confined.)

Influence 2 E.A.'s to not pursue completing their Degree by presenting them a book to read that contradicted Masonry and represented Masonry as being against the Bible.

Specification 2: In that the said Brother___Ford_____
                                Same as above Date
on or about the _____day of _____, 19___, at_____, did
    (State particulars as above outlined.)

Violate Article #506 Paragraph 2, Paragraph 9, Paragraph 10, and

Article #505 of the Laws of the Grand Lodge of Texas

(Other specifications, if any) _____

Dated ___21st. June _____, 1978.   _Leslie A. Wheeler_ m
                                             Worshipful Master   (To be signed by accuser.)
(If the Junior Warden signs the charges, he should do so officially. Charges should be delivered
           118
to the Secretary, who shall mark the same: "Filed this____21st____ day of _June_____,

1978, __Andrew V. Bean__ Secretary.")

THE STATE OF TEXAS:
COUNTY OF FORT BEND:

Before me, the undersigned authority, a Notary Public in and for said State and County, on this day personally

appeared _____ Arnold Finch _____ to me well known,
and known to me to be a credible person, who after being by me first sworn, on oath deposes and says as
follows; to wit:

My name is Arnold Finch, and I live at 123 First Street, Sugar Land, Texas.
In November of 1976, I petitioned the Sugar Land Masonic Lodge for the Degrees.
I was elected to receive the Degrees in December of 1976, and was initiationed
in January of 1977 for the First Degree.

In February of 1977, I went to the Ford Auto Supply to pick up some parts.
While I was there, the parts Store, Richard Ford, came up and asked me if I was
in the Lodge at Sugar Land. I told him that I was. Richard told me that he
had a book he wanted me to read and think about. The book was titled "Lodges
Against the Bible." It was written by some doctor, I do not call his name at
this time. I have known Richard for four years, and I know that it was Richard
Ford that gave me the book.

I told Jack Mercer that the book raised some questions about the Lodge that
I was unsure about, and did not know how to go about getting them answered.
Since that time I have talked to my father and other Master Masons, and would
like to re-petition the Lodge if possible.

I furthermore wish to state that if I still have the book and I can find it
I will be glad to turn it over to the Sugar Land Lodge $1141, for their use.

I also know that the Richard Ford that gave me this book "Lodges Against
the Bible," is the same Richard Ford that was a member of the Sugar Land Masonic
Lodge.

I furthermore wish to state that it was because of this book that I did not
further my Masonic education beyong the initiation, to the E. A. Degree.

I know the difference between right and wrong and the difference between the truth and a lie, and the above
statement is true and correct to the best of my knowledge and belief.

Witness my hand this the _____ 11th Day of December A. D. 19 78

_____ Arnold Ray Ford _____

Sworn and subscribed to before me this the __11th Day of December_____ A. D. 19_78

_____
Notary Public in and for Fort Bend County, Texas

136

CHAPTER FOURTEEN

POSSESSING THE LAND

A Master Mason in good standing who attended our church, went with me to the Masonic trial. They would allow only one Master Mason to enter with me. My pastor tried, but they wouldn't let him in. He sat in the front entrance hall and wouldn't budge. The guy who was supposed to be tending the door left it open because he was so frustrated by the presence of the pastor and the church people outside. Many Masons were turned away for lack of space to be seated within the Lodge.

There was a court reporter from Waco, Texas, a Grand Lodge Officer with his instrument for recording everything that transpired, and a prosecuting attorney who was a member of one of Houston's biggest Lodges.

Twelve men were on the jury. I was asked if I had presented a book titled **"Lodges Examined by the Bible"** to Entered Apprenticed Masons and other men of Masonry.

"Yes," I answered.

"Are you saying that you are guilty?"

"Yes, I am. I gave them the book."

They planned to treat me like some kind of criminal, but I would not allow it. I POSSESSED THIS LAND AND WENT IN AND CONTROLLED THE SITUATION IN THE NAME OF JESUS.

I approached the Master of the Lodge with all respect and said, "I will speak what God has told me to speak this day, and then I will leave and never return." He said, "Well, I guess we can give you five minutes, maybe ten, well, maybe fifteen. Well, whatever time you need, go ahead."

Satan whispered to me that I had taken a vow to have my throat cut, my body torn open and that it would come to pass - everything I had - my home, children, everything would fall.

But I knew the Word of God. I had become strong in it, so I stood and quoted the Scriptures. You had better know how to stand on the Word because the enemy will destroy you if you do not know the Word of God. **You'd better have it down in your heart and not just in your mind**.

Before I could go into the Lodge I had to put on the whole armor of God. Daily I must walk in it. Why? So I can be able to stand against the wiles of the devil when he comes against me. We don't wrestle with flesh and blood - if that had been the case I could have whipped him before the trial. (Ephesians 6:10-18)

I carried the Word of God into the Lodge with me, praying with all prayer and supplications in the spirit.

I went in and possessed the land. The Bible says in James 1:5: *"If any of you lack wisdom, let him ask of God, that giveth to all men liberally, and upbraideth not; and it shall be given him."* I asked - God gave! I walked in there knowing what they were going to try to do, and was already prepared by God to outsmart them, outmaneuver them, and do whatever needed to be done to bring glory to God.

I'd been given permission to speak. With my Bible in hand I said, "Masonry is not against the Bible. **The Bible, the Word of God**, which is without fault or error, **is against the Masonic Order as an organization, not the men in it**. God and His Son Jesus loves everyone. The Bible is taken for granted by Masonry. The Lodge teaches that you only have to believe in a deity (a Supreme Being) not God." I read from the **Lodge Manual**,

THE FURNITURE OF THE LODGE

"The Holy Bible, Square and Compass are said to constitute the *furniture of the lodge*. They are, respectively dedicated to God; to the Master of the Lodge; and to the Craft. The Holy Bible is properly called a greater light of Masonry, for from the center of the Lodge it pours forth from east to west and north to south its effulgent rays and divine truth. The Bible is used, among Masons in this country, as the symbol of the Will of God, however it may be expressed; and, therefore, whatever expresses that Will may be used as a substitute for the Bible in other countries; otherwise, Masonry would be a sectarian instituting, incapable of universality. Thus, in a Lodge consisting entirely of Jews, the Old Testament alone may be placed upon the altar. Turkish Masons may make use of the Koran. Whether it be the Gospel to the Christian, the Pentateuch to the Israelite, The Koran to the Mussulman, or the Vedas to the Braham, it everywhere Masonically conveys *the same idea*-that the symbolism of the Divine Will revealed to man. . ." [18]

I continued, "However, the Bible teaches there is only one God, one Son, and one Holy Spirit. To be a part of Masonry means you agree with the whole concept of the order. There are Muslims, Hindus and other Masons that **deny Jesus Christ is the Son of God**.

140

II Corinthians 6: 14-18 teaches *'Be ye not unequally yoked together with unbelievers: for what fellowship hath righteousness with unrighteousness? And what communion hath light with darkness? And what concord hath Christ with Belial? Or what part hath he that believeth with an infidel? And what agreement hath the temple of God with idols? for ye are the temple of the living God; as God hath said, I will dwell in them, and walk in them; and I will be their God, and they will be my people. Wherefore come out from among them, and be ye separate, saith the Lord, and touch not the unclean thing; and I will receive you, and will be a Father unto you, And ye shall be my sons and daughters, saith the Lord Almighty.'"*

"Also it says in Ephesians 5: 11-12, *'And have no fellowship with the unfruitful works of darkness, but rather reprove them. For it is a shame even to speak of those things which are done of them in secret.'"*

"The Lodge keeps secrets from the world about the order sworn by oath. It binds Lodge members together above all others, and that they are never to reveal the secrets of the Lodge. Even forbidding the husband to tell his wife - whom God has put together as one flesh. This causes division between many husbands and wives. It is secret in that it binds a man to never tell on another Mason if he sees him committing a crime. The secret oath that he has taken before God that his body, the temple of the Holy Ghost, shall be destroyed by having his tongue torn out, his heart and vitals ripped out, his body severed in twain - is not of God."

"The Lodge discriminates against races. James 2:9 says, *'But if ye have respect to persons, ye commit sin, and are convinced of the law as transgressors."* God is not a respecter of persons!

II John 9, *'Whosoever transgresseth, and abideth not in the doctrine of Christ, hath not God. He that abideth in the doctrine of Christ, he hath both the Father and the Son'.* "The Lodge never prays in the name of Jesus. In my years in this organization I've never heard the name of Jesus Christ mentioned, yet that Name rules and reigns this universe. Philippians 2: 10 - 11 says, *'That at the name of Jesus every knee should bow, of things in heaven, and things in earth, and things under the earth; And that every tongue should confess that Jesus Christ is Lord, to the glory of God the Father.'*

"The Lodge teaches salvation by good character and works all done through self, carnal effort, when the Word of God says that Christ is our righteousness."

"The Lodge recognizes the god of Muhammadans and others who deny Christ. This is idolatry."

"The Lodge calls man 'Worshipful Master'. Only Jesus is to be worshiped and to be the master of men. *'Neither be ye called master for one is your master, even Christ'*, (Matthew 23:10). Jesus said in Matthew 15: 8-9, *'This people draweth nigh unto me with their mouth, and honoureth me with their lips; but their heart is far from me. But in vain they do worship me, teaching for doctrines the commandments of men.'* Joshua 24: 15 tells us *'And if it seem evil unto you to serve the Lord, choose you this day whom ye will serve; . . . but as for me and my house, we will serve the Lord.'"*

"The Lodge requires total loyalty to its oaths and system. Yet the Scripture teaches that we are to forsake all other allegiances and to worship but one God and the Savior, Jesus."

"I respect each man in this Lodge, and all men because Jesus commands us to do so. I'm not against any man, but I am against the Masonic organization and any religion or organization that stands between God and man. I love you, but more important, God loves you and gave His Son for your salvation."

"Gentlemen, let Jesus Christ into your heart and get out of the Lodge. I closed by quoting Acts 4: 19-20, 29 "... *Whether it be right in the sight of God to hearken unto you more than unto God, judge ye. For we cannot but speak the things which we have seen and heard...And now, Lord, behold their threatenings: and grant unto thy servants, that with all boldness they may speak thy word, by stretching forth thine hand to heal; and that signs and wonders may be done by the name of thy holy child Jesus.'"*

I closed my Bible. I personally knew almost every one there. One of the men who sat in judgment on me had encouraged me to get involved in the church. Some were my teachers in school, many were business associates. They knew me BEFORE, they knew me DURING, and they knew me AFTER I had become involved in the Lodge.

I went to the Master of the Lodge, shook his hand and looked straight in his eyes and said, "I love you and God loves you." I walked around the room and did that to every man in the room. Many of them wept openly. Some of them gnashed their teeth.

I walked out of there with the boldness and victory of Jesus Christ. I then went to San Marcos to teach a Bible study. My life was never the same. Once again I was thrust into a walk of faith that I never knew existed. It is one thing to know the Word of God, to speak it, but it is another thing to live it and to be able to stand on and use it in everyday life.

Needless to say, I received a notice in the mail from

the Grand Lodge of the State of Texas. It read: **NO-TICE OF SUSPENSION OR EXPULSION FOR UNMASONIC CONDUCT**. I was expelled from the Masonic Order. In their eyes I'm not fit to ever be a Mason again. In fact, in their eyes I am dead.

Some years later a UPS delivery man was delivering a package to our church. My secretary was inviting him to church and casually asked "Do you know Richard Ford?" "Yes", he replied, "He's dead!" "Dead?", proclaimed my secretary with astonishment. At that very moment I stepped into the building and was passing by her desk. She looked up and proclaimed, "Look there's the dead man you're talking about!"

Why did this man think me to be dead? He was a Mason! A member of Sugar Land Lodge #1141. He had seen my picture hanging on the wall of the Lodge with all past Worshipful Masters. But, mine was different. A black drape covered my picture. To him and all others who would see my picture they would be reminded, ".... that there might not remain among men or Masons trace or recollection of so vile a wretch as I...".

I was called before the council for preaching and teaching the Word of God - I count it an honor.

I've often thought about that day and the verdict of

'guilty'. I continually ask myself and others, "If you were brought to trial, accused of being a Christian, accused of causing sedation among religious folk, accused of being a ring leader, accused of being a pestilent fellow and turning the world upside down, would we be found guilty or not guilty? **Thank God - I am guilty!** And I have been ....

SET FREE!

---

18 - L.M.L. - pg 217

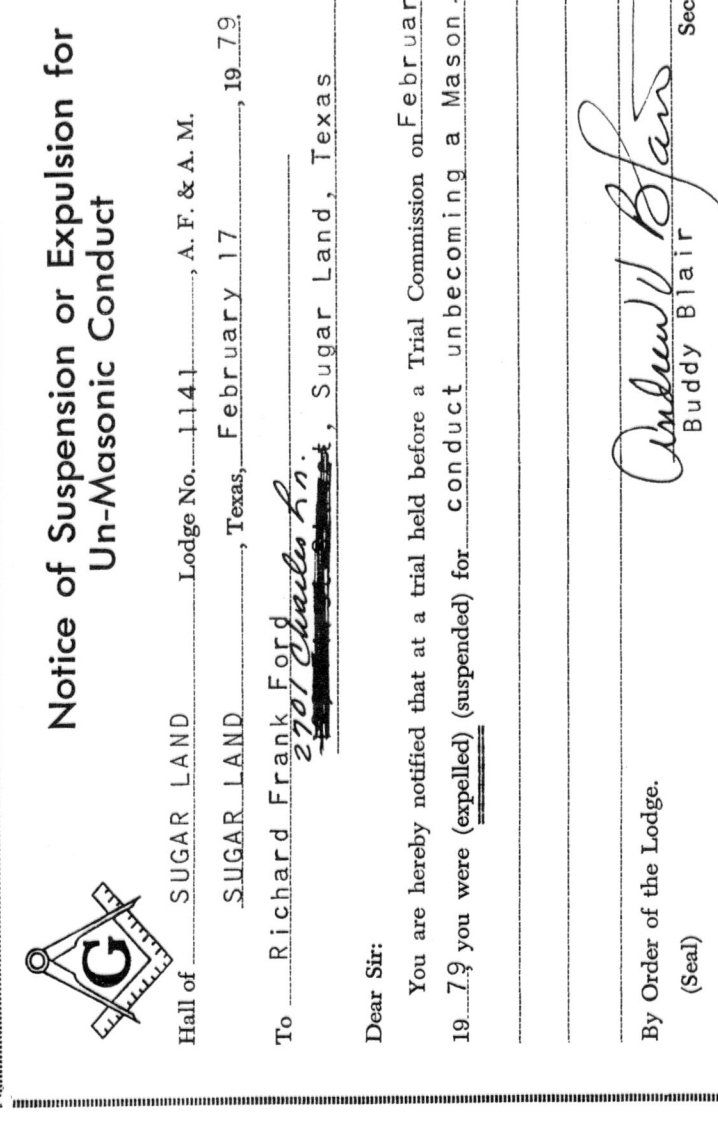

Notice of Suspension or Expulsion for Un-Masonic Conduct

Hall of ____SUGAR LAND____ Lodge No. ____1141____, A. F. & A. M.

____SUGAR LAND____, Texas, ____February 17____, 19_79_.

To ____Richard Frank Ford____
____2701 Charles Ln.____, Sugar Land, Texas

Dear Sir:

You are hereby notified that at a trial held before a Trial Commission on ____February 17____, 19_79_, you were (expelled) (suspended) for ____conduct unbecoming a Mason.____

By Order of the Lodge.

(Seal)

Buddy Blair
____Secretary.____

Form No. 13—150—3-72   Masonic Home Press

CHAPTER FIFTEEN

CONCLUSION

During my final review of the manuscript, I found that "Lighfoot's Manual of the Lodge" had been replaced with "Monitor of the Lodge."

In reviewing the "Monitor of the Lodge", I noted that all the commentaries by Jewel P. Lightfoot had been deleted.

These commentaries contained explanations in detail of the historical foundation of Masonry and how it is interwoven with ancient cult worship. Drawing much of its symbolism and ceremonies from ancient Egyptian culture as well as interweaving the religious ceremonies of Mohammedans, Druids, Hinduism, Buddhism, etc. All of which was veiled with biblical practices and beliefs. Thus arriving at the most dangerous of mixtures which produced the Angel of Light, the Master of deception.

Then I noted that the recommendation to revise "Lightfoot's Manual of the Lodge" began in earnest in December, 1978 and was submitted to the Grand Lodge for adoption at the 1980 Grand Annual Communications, with copyright in 1982. It's interesting to note that my conflict with the Lodge began at this same time and ended with my expulsion in 1979. You don't suppose that God used me and my encounter to shake the Lodge to its foundation, causing it to retreat, regroup and rebuild - do you?

Remember what Paul said in II Corinthians 2:11 *"Lest Satan should get an advantage of us: For we are not ignorant of his devices."*

Know this, an enemy that has not been totally destroyed will retreat, regroup, rebuild and then will return.

It is evident Satan retreated, regrouped, rebuilt and returned with a new covering. Yet, he is still masquerading as an Angel of Light, seeking whom he may deceive, devour and place in bondage.

". . . you will know the truth and the truth will set you free" 19

The truth has been presented to you to the best of my knowledge and ability, and with all the sincerity of my heart. I have not sought to degrade any man, but to lift the name of Jesus. You have been shown that the enemy has used the Masonic Organization and its many branches to deceive the world. Multitudes are in bondage and must be SET FREE.

The Bible says that in the last days many false prophets, doctrines and teachings of men shall come forth. (I Timothy 4:1) We are in the last days, Jesus Christ is coming soon. Are you ready? Are you prepared to meet the Savior of the world, Jesus? If not, invite Him to come into your heart.

If you are ready to make peace with God and to ask Jesus to save you, pray this prayer.

God, I come to you a sinner, I know I am separated from you because of my sins. Forgive me! Jesus, I believe you are the Son of God; I believe you came to this earth, born of a virgin by the power of the Holy Ghost; lived a sinless life; freely gave your life for me. My sins against God cried for justice, a penalty had to be paid. Thank you for paying the price for my sins, it cost your life. You died for me that I could be free. Thank you! Jesus, you were declared to be the Son of God on the day you resurrected from the dead. Today I am a child of God. My faith is in the finished work of God through Jesus Christ. Amen!

If you are one of the many thousands who are involved in Freemasonry, or any of its branch organizations, I would encourage you to pray. God will release you from the bondage of Masonry.

Pray this prayer:

Father, I come in the name of Jesus Christ. I had no knowledge or wisdom of the things involved in the Masonic Lodge (or branch organizations). I had no knowledge that they were an evil organization. I saw that they spoke of goodness and godliness but discovered they were not of You. I come asking that You forgive me. I renounce Masonry (or branch organizations) in the name of Jesus. I renounce the bondage of the oath of obligation that I repeated when I was made a Mason (or branch organizations that I belong to). I realize it is not of You. Father God, forgive me. I thank You that I stand before You now clean and pure because I have seen the truth, and the truth has made me free. I thank you for it in Jesus name.

"If the Son therefore shall make you free, ye shall be free indeed." (John 8:36)

Believe in your heart that God has truly set you free. Remember the Scriptures that tell us to have no fellowship with the unfruitful works of darkness. Abstain from the appearance of evil, as the Word instructs. Resist the devil, and he will flee from you - he has to do that when you've submitted yourself to God. Stay away from all secret organizations, and works of darkness.

I pray that the material in this book will not be used to condemn those who may be involved in Masonry or its many branches. God does not condemn. Present them a copy of this book. The truth will convict them and set them free. Sincerely pray for those you know who are in bondage. God will do the rest. They will be . . .

SET FREE!

---

19 - The Amplified Bible - Zondervan Bible Publishers - John 8:32

RICHARD FORD

Richard Ford is a God-called and seasoned Pastor, who along with his wife, Tena, have pastored Family Worship Center in Stafford, Texas since 1980. His heart stirring messages are changing the lives of many each day. Those that know him have said; he has the obedience of Abraham, the spirit of Joseph, the faithfulness of Paul, the submission of Timothy, the power of the Holy Ghost, and the compassion of Jesus, as he reaches out to the world.

He preaches the Word of God with a "Holy Ghost Fire" that transforms its hearers forever. He's Hell's greatest nightmare, yet, the father-like compassion of Christ is imparted from him to men, women, and children during their most desperate time of need.

Pastor Ford's heart's desire is to train and to equip members of the Body of Christ to become all that God purposes for them to be. His heart to win the lost is evident in his sermons and also in his calling to the foreign soils of the world where he has preached to the multitudes.